Liliana Ponce

Theory of the Voice and Dream

translated from Spanish by Michael Martin Shea

 WORLD POETRY

Theory of the Voice and Dream
Copyright © Liliana Ponce, 2025
English translation copyright © Michael Martin Shea, 2025

The works included in this book were originally published by tsé-tsé in Buenos Aires, Argentina as *Teoría de la voz y el sueño* (2001) and *Fudekara* (2008)

First Edition, First Printing, 2025
ISBN 978-1-954218-33-8

World Poetry Books
New York, NY
www.worldpoetrybooks.com

Available to the trade through Asterism Books
Distributed in the UK and Europe by Turnaround Publisher Services
Subscriptions and standing orders available directly from the publisher

Library of Congress Control Number: 2025930688

Cover design by Andrew Bourne
Typesetting by Don't Look Now
Printed in Lithuania by BALTO Print

World Poetry Books is a 501(c)(3) nonprofit and charitable organization founded in 2017 in New York City, affiliated with the Humanities Institute and the Translation Program at the University of Connecticut (Storrs), and a member of the Community of Literary Magazines and Presses (CLMP).

World Poetry's publications and programs are made possible with funding from the Poetry Foundation and the New York State Council on the Arts, as well as generous support from individual donors and subscribers.

Table of Contents

Translator's Introduction   vii

The Somber Season   19

Beyond the Somber Season   31

Only the Eye Sees Blue   51

Knowledge Scatters the Body   67

Diary   87

Other Poems   129

    Love in Oceans of Sand   131

    Psyche and Eros   143

    Allegory of the Morning   149

    House as Kingdom   155

Fudekara   165

Acknowledgments   197

Translator's Introduction

Theory of the Voice and Dream begins where most poets would leave off. The collection's first line—"Escribir es hoy un vacío," or, "To write today is an emptiness"—may seem like the prelude to a retreat, or a Bartlebian refusal. But for Liliana Ponce, absence and lack serve as the generative preconditions for the creative act. The poem goes on, writing continues: emptiness is not a terminus, much less a failure, but something else—a possibility, a temptation. A void that holds the poet in its orbit.

In 2015, I was on a bus from Buenos Aires to La Plata, Argentina when I read these opening lines of *Teoría de la voz y el sueño*, Ponce's 2001 collection. It was a winter's day, bright but not warm, the undersaturated light seeming to meld with the dull grass along the highway. Emptiness in the passage, emptiness in the form. I was far from home, wherever that was, and felt I knew exactly what she meant.

Theory of the Voice and Dream unites Ponce's two most widely circulated collections: the aforementioned book from which this volume draws its name, and the slim follow-up, *Fudekara*, which appeared in 2008. Published by Reynaldo Jiménez's legendary tsé-tsé imprint, together these two books inaugurated the poet's mid-career turn: the meditative and philosophical lyric sequences for which she is most well-known. Indeed, the metapoetic opening line of the collection sketches in miniature the concerns that haunt all of Ponce's mature work: the absence that animates the act of creation, the gap between word and thing, the limits of language as it stretches asymptotically toward the real. Her title is more than simply evocative; what Ponce offers in her stark, nimble lines is a vision of *poesis*, a creative method balanced on the precipice of refusal, which draws strength from twinned sources: the oneiric and the oral, the vatic and the intimate.

Liliana Ponce was born in Buenos Aires in 1950. She studied literature and completed postgraduate work in linguistics and semiotics at the University of Buenos Aires. She developed an interest in Japanese literature and drama, including Noh theater, and studied meditation, Buddhism, and other religious practices, all of which influenced her poetic work.

Ponce's debut collection—*Trama continua* ("Continuous Weft"), which was awarded the 1974 prize in poetry by the Fondo Nacional de las Artes—also bore the significant influence of Alejandra Pizarnik, taking up and extending the great poet's neo-surrealist project through what would become Ponce's defining formal choice, the serial poem. The three long sections of *Trama continua* inaugurated Ponce's habit of composing and publishing individual lyric poems in extended, numbered sequences, where images and phrases repeat and reverberate. Her second volume, *Composición: Poesía 1976–1979*, was published a decade later (though, as the title indicates, the poems were written shortly after her debut publication and share a similar aesthetic). The book was released by Último Reino, a press known for its promotion of the neoromantic school of poetry, an important precursor for what would become the broader Latin American aesthetic of the *neobarroco*, or neobaroque.

The seventeen-year interregnum between *Composición* and *Teoría de la voz y el sueño* could be seen as a long period of silence, a reading which finds analogical support in Ponce's increasing focus on moments of stillness, a kind of poetic rendering of the meditative and religious practices she had studied for decades. Yet during the late 1980s and 1990s, Ponce wrote (and still writes) incessantly. In the closing decade of the 20th century, her poems appeared in literary journals both in Argentina and abroad. Some of these were later found in the two books collected here; others came from manuscripts with titles like *Vaca Antropofagia* ("Cow Cannibalism")[1] that have yet to see the light of day. Ponce has often remarked in interviews that she has mountains of drafts that have never been published.[2] For her, writing is an end in itself, a self-contained practice only tangentially related to publishing. Her interest in calendrical forms, for instance—evidenced most strongly in *Fudekara* and the long sequence "Diario" in this book—has its root in her long-standing practice of keeping a daily journal.

Teoría de la voz y el sueño thus emerges not from a period of quiet contemplation, but from a rigorous writing habit. Where in her early volumes, the lyric voice fractures across half-glimpsed images to stretch gender, time, and space, here her hallmark serial method is applied with more conceptual aims, using the image as a sort of mental-industrial lubricant to drill down into the chasms between a thing and its likeness, between what's spoken and what is. Yet the majesty of Ponce's work lies in her delicate balancing act, where such high-level abstraction veers into flashes of almost quotidian imagery, brief as cloudbursts. It is this movement which gives the collection its power and builds its implicit theory of aesthetics.

Her subsequent volume, the brief *Fudekara*—whose title is a transliteration of two Japanese terms meaning "from the brush"—is Ponce's most famous and frequently anthologized work. Originally composed in 1993 over the course of a 14-day calligraphy class, the poems originate from the speaker's hand in motion as she traces lines in ink, using this repeated movement as a point of departure for larger questions about the relationship between self and text. In its concision and emphasis on the materiality of the writing process, *Fudekara* thus operates as a kind of skeleton key for Ponce's entire poetic project. As Jorge Monteleone, editor of the canon-shaping anthology *200 años de poesía Argentina*, describes it, Ponce's work is most notable for how it conceives of writing as "an alternative register of the real."[3] This sense of the poem as a *register*, as something in progress, evolving dialectically with the amorphous real, marks Ponce's work as experimental in the most literal sense of the word. The poems are experiments, their meditative, serial character less an arbitrary aesthetic form than a cognitive one, a unique mode of thought itself.

Such an approach has won her the admiration of her contemporaries, even as it has marked her work as distinct from major poetic currents of the national and regional scenes. As scholar Martín Prieto notes, Argentine poetry in the closing decades of the twentieth century took shape around a series of dyads.[4] Young poets in the early 1980s turned against the *culto* (highbrow, literary, or mannered) poetry of figures like Juan Gelman, writing poems that were messy, playful, and profane. This bubbling of energy coalesced into what is now known as the neobaroque, an aesthetic whose general orientation is perhaps best captured by Argentine neobaroque poet Néstor Perlongher's renaming of the movement as the *neobarroso*, or neo-filth.[5] Gaudy and excessive (or, in the eyes of its detractors, sloppy and unrestrained), the neobaroque was an international movement, drawing on and in figures from across the Americas, like Brazilian poet Haroldo de Campos and Cuban writer Severo Sarduy.

The ascendency of the neobaroque in turn produced dissatisfaction among a new group of younger poets, primarily located in Buenos Aires, who were interested in returning poetry to its documentarian function and recovering everyday language.[6] The resulting *objetivismo* movement, led by figures such as Daniel Samoilovich and Fabián Casas, spawned its own network of little magazines and reading series with an ambiguous relation to the neobaroque. As both Prieto and Edgardo Dobry note, the neobaroque-objectivist binary is relatively limited. *Objetivismo* is often figured as the domestic reaction to the neobaroque's international assemblage, but its practitioners were largely schooled in U.S. Objectivism of the early twentieth century. Moreover, both sides claimed complex precursor figures like Juan L. Ortiz and Léonidas Lamborghini as their own. Nevertheless, tensions between partisans of opaque and plain-spoken language animated poetic debates and production around the turn of the century.

Yet such a framework struggles to accommodate Ponce's work, despite her association with the neobaroque—a connection foisted on her primarily due to her publishers' affiliations. Jiménez's tsé-tsé imprint inherited the mantle of the neoromantic/neobaroque legacy from Último Reino, sharing many of the earlier press's roster of collaborators. Jiménez himself appeared in the pages of the seminal anthology of the neobaroque, *Medusario*, alongside future tsé-tsé authors (and Ponce's future pressmates) José Kozer, Roberto Echavarren, and Néstor Perlongher. But Ponce's poetry, even in its earliest iterations, never took up the gaudy and excessive linguistic maximalism for which the *neobarroco* was known; neither are her poems particularly plain-spoken or given to documentarian impulses, even when they start with an ostensible scene. As in *Fudekara*, the "real" (often figured as the act of writing) is minutely attended to, yet also serves as a launchpad for dreams and meditations, ones which take the poet from the surreal to the conceptual, and in which writing itself extends beyond death and time. In this, the singularity of her aesthetic vision marks her as a pivotal (if still underappreciated) figure in the history of Argentine—and, indeed, American—poetics.

Argentine literature frequently asks to be read within its notably vexed national historical context, which articulates itself around two key moments in the late twentieth and early twenty-first centuries: first, the military dictatorship ("el proceso de reorganización nacional," or simply "el proceso") that ruled the country from 1976 to 1983 following a period of intense political violence, and which was responsible for brutal human rights violations; second, the economic and social collapse of 2001. These twin crises—connected through the dictatorship's economic policies and, indeed, the broader question of national economic development—came on the heels of a longer history of political instability in a nation that saw six military coups in the twentieth century alone. The antinomies, then, between

Perlongher and *culto* figures like Juan Gelman, or between the neobaroque and the younger *objetivismo* poets of the 1990s, are rooted not only in a local history of literary antagonisms dating back to (at least) the Florida-Boedo divide in Argentine modernism of the 1920s, but also in a nearly omnipresent and urgent debate about the relationship between artist and society, one which has generated conflicting schools of thought.

Yet an over-reliance on political violence as an explanatory framework for Southern Cone poetics has stunted our understanding of the plurality of aesthetics and poetries in the region. As scholar Ben Bollig has noted, the practice of translation—including the selection of texts and the framing of paratextual materials—is shot through with ideological vectors, particularly so in the case of regions where the U.S. provided diplomatic and military support for repressive governments.[7] Bollig points to the widely translated figure of Gelman, himself a militant before going into exile during the dictatorship, as indicative of this problem, evidenced in the centering of Gelman's period of militancy in the packaging of his translations by U.S. translators and editors. This tendency to substitute political activism or militancy as a metric for translatability risks reducing the complex intellectual and aesthetic currents in Argentine society to epiphenomenal renderings of political histories. Indeed, Gelman himself is a far stranger poet than his widely translated and anthologized poems might suggest—he was not only a militant who lived in exile from an oppressive right-wing regime, but was also the inventor of various literary heteronyms, a kind of midcentury Pessoa in his own right.[8]

Ponce's poems collected here stage neither the violence of the military junta nor the crisis that opened the twenty-first century. Other poems take up these issues, albeit obliquely; *Trama continua*'s surreal and fragmented lyrics are marked by the presence of corpses, particularly portentous in the context of the political violence of the early 1970s, while "Urbs dixit," a rare standalone poem written in the aftermath of the 2001 collapse, is composed entirely of found text taken from newspaper reports about the crisis. But in this volume, the focus is inward, even if the questions the poems raise—of gender and desire, creation and escape—are necessarily directed back outward in a dialectical loop. In this, *Theory of the Voice and Dream* offers a corrective to a canon of poetry in translation that has oversimplified the types of poems being written in the Southern Cone.

The fact that Ponce is a woman is also not incidental, as the question of gender is particularly salient both domestically within Argentina and for world literary translation markets. As Prieto notes, the neobaroque-objectivism binary tends to obscure how the 1980s and 1990s were a period that saw an unprecedented number of collections published by female poets and authors in South America, bucking entrenched publishing norms. Even still, only three of the 22 writers included in the aforementioned *Medusario* anthology of 1996 were women, replicating an old pattern in which poetic movements were dominated by men. Ponce's turn-of-the-century work was part of this effusion of new publications by women. The work of some of her contemporaries—including María Negroni, Mirta Rosenberg, and Susana Villalba—has since begun to appear in English. Hopefully more will follow.

Beyond the book's historical importance and its relevance to issues of representation, however, there is the work itself—Ponce's singularly beautiful lines wrought from a deep understanding of the relationship between word and image, mouth and voice. Living inside *Teoría...* and *Fudekara* for the past decade has been a privilege and a gift, one I'm grateful to share.

I began translating Liliana Ponce's work in earnest in 2016, beginning with the poems from *Fudekara*, and in particular, "Día 3," a poem whose repeating line—"desambulaba por la ciudad de tu mapa"—had rattled around in my head throughout my time in South America the previous year. This project was my first serious attempt at literary translation, and in many ways translating Ponce's work was an education in the art of translation itself. The book's long incubation allowed me to glimpse what I feel to be the nature of translation in its extremity, as the experience of a trance. The decisions I made throughout this volume were informed by my familiarity with Ponce's broader body of work, conversations with the author herself, and untold hours with various dictionaries. But at its heart, translation for me is the experience of surrendering my language to another's, of Ponce's work speaking through me.

Some of the challenges presented by this project included learning how to balance Ponce's tendency for abstraction without losing the musicality of her language, how to maintain the strangeness of her verse, her patterns of association, and the quick shifts to the unknown, while preserving the fluidity of her lyric voice. As is often the case in Romance-language poetry, Ponce's lines have an inherent music borne of common word endings. Where such music cannot be maintained without significantly altering how the poem thinks, I have sought to re-create it at another place in the poem, as a kind of echo. In the opening poem, for instance, the final stanza features an emphatic rhyme between "estilo" and "vacío," one impossible to re-create with the given options in English ("style" and "emptiness.") But English offers other routes to such music, including the one I took, where the rhyme is found by way of the cognates "horror" and "ochre," the latter re-arranged in the final line's list of adjectives.

One particularly challenging passage appears in the opening lines of "Allegory of the Morning," where the irresistible rhyme of "un rayo de luz," a ray of light, and the name of the seventeenth-century English poet, Thomas Carew, was too good to lose, and yet could not be accommodated by English. So I let the line stand in Spanish, as a testament to how, for Ponce, the poem's particular form of cognition relies on its unique sonic and associative technologies—the music of the voice, the rush of the dream.

Notes

1 "Antropofagia" or "cannibalism" should be read as a reference to the Brazilian *movimento antropofágico*, or cannibalist movement, of the 1920s, a poetic movement advanced primarily by Oswald de Andrade. De Andrade used the trope of cannibalism to argue that colonized nations should voraciously consume—and thus transform—the culture of the colonizer.

2 See, for instance: Silvia Guerra, "Entrevista a Liliana Ponce: La lengua, ese abismo del mundo," *Hispanic Poetry Review* 11, no. 6 (2016): 101–109.

3 Jorge Monteleone, "Prólogo," in *200 años de poesía Argentina*, edited by Jorge Monteleone (Buenos Aires: Alfaguara, 2010), 25. All translations mine.

4 See: Martín Prieto, *Breve historia de la literatura Argentina* (Buenos Aires: Taurus, 2003), 447–454.

5 See: Perlongher's introduction ("Prólogo: Neobarroco y neobarroso") to the canon-shaping anthology, *Medusario: Muestra de la poesía latinoamericana*, edited by Roberto Echavarren, Jacobo Sefamí, and José Kozer (Mexico City: Fondo de Cultura Económica, 1996), 19–30.

6 On *objetivismo*, see: Prieto, ibid., 452–454. See also: Edgardo Dobry, "Poesía argentina actual: del neobarroco al objetivismo," *Cuadernos Hispanoamericanos*, 588 (1999): 45–57; Jorge Fondebrider, "Treinta años de poesía argentina," *INTI: Revista de literatura hispánica*, 52–53 (2000): 5–32.

7 Ben Bollig, "Recent English Translations of Poetry from Argentina: Contexts and Strategies," *Translation and Literature*, 25, no. 1 (2016): 107–130.

8 See, for instance: Juan Gelman, *The Poems of Sydney West*, trans. Katherine M. Hedeen and Víctor Rodríguez Núñez (Cromer, UK: Salt Publishing, 2009). For a critical study on Gelman's heteronymic translations, see: Olivia Lott, "In/Subordination: Pseudo/Translation and the Cultural Cold War in Juan Gelman's *The Poems of Sydney West*," *PMLA*, 138, no. 3 (2023): 534–550.

Theory of the Voice and Dream

La estación sombría

The Somber Season

1.

Escribir es hoy un vacío —está en la forma
o el pasaje, en un trozo sin pertenencia:
máxima intensidad, duración.
¿Estará aquí el oscuro tópico, la sombra
toda veladura, armando y quitando
las telas sin expresión de una nube?
Reprobación del maestro—
descorre la ventana, se suceden los días.

Escribir es hoy un vacío.
Por elección, no buscaré más que la tradición de la mano
consagrada a la cera, la gradual decadencia.

El pasaje fantasmal y el punto neutro estallan con horror
—inexistencia de un estilo.
Ya no yo, ni antes—
Escribir es hoy un vacío, ocre, acre.

1.

To write today is an emptiness—it's in the form
or the passage, in a piece without belonging:
maximum intensity, duration.
Will we find the dark subject here, the shadow
totally glazed, assembling and removing
the expressionless threads of a cloud?
Teacher's reproach—
draw open the window, the days go on.

To write today is an emptiness.
By choice, I will look no further than the tradition of the hand
blessed by wax, the gradual decline.

The ghostly passage and the neutral point burst with horror
—absence of a style.
No longer me, nor before—
To write today is an emptiness, bitter, ochre.

2.

Quedaré en la arena real,
la forma tangible de una piedra,
en la transmutación del azar hecha con el aliento.

Con palabras alimento la creación del tiempo
—otro puede escribir, otro puede hablar.
Movimientos líquidos transitados por la médula
de un cuerpo falso.
El vidrio absorbe el cielo.

Quedaré en la arena, en el polvo de la piedra
—en lo oscuro de la aridez los borro.
Tranquilízame con la pasividad.
Tranquilízame porque no existo.

2.

I will wait in the real sand,
the tangible form of rock,
in the conversion of fate by breath.

With words I feed the creation of time
—someone else can speak, someone else can write.
Liquid movements cycled by the marrow
of a false body.
The glass absorbs the sky.

I will wait in the sand, in the dust of the rock
—in the shadow of dryness I erase them.
Soothe me with passive thoughts.
Soothe me because I don't exist.

3.

Son las ocho de la noche
sobre el agua del acuario
—día inacabado en el transcurso de la arena.
Lo que se espera del aire es un sueño que no sabe
el tejido de sombras.

Día inacabado sobre el transcurso de la arena
como tus ojos, como mi mirada.

Aquí está la sed de los impulsos,
la playa sin memoria donde hablan las semejanzas,
y aun así, hermanas, se deshacen en los espejismos,
como tus ojos, como mi mirada.

Las palabras acontecen más allá del objeto
roídas de tragedia antigua y de risa vacía,
desborden desde las hojas sus costados.

La tierra buscada quema los labios
a las ocho de la noche sobre el vidrio del acuario.
Lejos del pensamiento tu ojo plegado, las voces lejos.

3.

It's eight at night
over the aquarium water
—unending day in the passage of sand.
What you want from air is a dream
unschooled in the fabric of shadows.

Unending day above the passage of sand,
like your eyes, my gaze.

Here is the thirst of impulses,
beach without memory where likenesses speak,
and even so, sisters, they dissolve in mirages,
like your eyes, my gaze.

Beyond the object words are
gnawed by ancient tragedy and empty laughs,
splitting their sides from the page.

The desired earth burns the lips,
eight at night over the aquarium glass.
Far from thinking your folded eye, the voices distant.

4.

Las cosas suceden de otro modo—
el nacimiento, ese largo modo sin habitación, en el que ya no puedo
   hurgar,
el tiempo, rodeándome poco a poco,
sobre el ojo descarnado en torno a mi mano, el cuello, la boca,
para no permanecer sino hacerme doblar, más aún,
desde este gesto que me hace semejante a tu raíz.

Pero no es eso lo que queda por añadir
sino la palabra desprovista ahora de sangre y sed.
Insípido, oscuro —es desde ese lugar que no me requiere:
tolera, succiona,
y convierte a la calma en debilidad precoz.
Es esa mudez que me busca,
se liga a mi cuerpo.

A la luz del día, a la sombra asida,
sin la quietud de la piedra, atada todavía a la memoria,
indicio en el reposo, ardor en ese cambio que lleva
de un momento a otro
y se entierra en el hielo
—diente o jiba que me llaman.

Las cosas suceden de otro modo.
No he dado nada:
las estrellas en la tormenta, la palabra en el bacín.

Y ésta que espía, en trance de expirar,
sopa fétida en la órbita de otra noche,
viene y cae—
no vuelta al revés, sino precediéndote.

4.

Things happen in other ways—
birth, that long form without a room, in which I can no longer
 rummage,
time, surrounding me little by little,
above the brutal eye encircling my hand, throat, mouth,
not to stay close but to fold me, more still,
with this gesture which casts me as your origin.

Yet this is not what remains to be added
but rather the word now barren of blood and thirst.
Insipid, dark—it's from that place I'm not required:
it bears, it suckles,
and turns the calm to precocious weakness.
It's the silence that searches for me,
tying itself to my body.

In the daylight, in the anchored shadow,
without the rock's stillness, still weighted to memory,
a sign in the repose, passion in the change that moves
from one moment to another
and buries itself in the ice
—tooth or hump that they call me.

Things happen in other ways.
I've given nothing:
the stars in the storm, the word in the basin.

And this that spies, at the risk of expiring,
fetid soup in the orbit of another night,
it comes and falls—
not spun around, but gone before you.

5.

Cuerpos rígidos como ramas se desploman
para liberarse del primer sueño,
buscar en el agua turbia la imagen
arrollándose en una cortina de algas
o buscar lo imperfecto en lo desnudo
para escribir —el límite es la elección de la noche.

En la punta del hilo: rayo o serpiente.
Es el hilo que ata el amanecer a los cuerpos
después que rígidos se desploman.

La borrosa luz que ensancha los contornos,
mar de todas las máscaras,
es el vaso que recoge tu materia.

5.

Rigid bodies like branches collapse
to free themselves from the first dream,
to search in turbid waters for the image
rolling in a curtain of algae
or to seek the imperfect in the naked
in order to write—the night decides the limit.

On the tip of the thread: serpent or lightning.
It's the thread that ties dawn to the bodies,
once they, rigid, collapse.

The blurry light that widens the borders,
ocean of all of the masks,
is the glass that collects your matter.

Más allá de la estación sombría

Beyond the Somber Season

1.

Abre la puerta la bestia y tiembla
—cuando vuelva
me rodearé de helechos
y haré del aire sangre y linfa.
La pesada piel se habrá disuelto
al abrir la puerta la bestia.

Me alzo en el sueño y lo repito, sin voluntad,
como era en la inmovilidad de la piedra.

La ola sale del ojo, de la tierra abierta
—arrojo lascivos susurros.

La voz es la sombra, es el cuerpo.
Razón, punto de luz,
cae derrumbado el árbol de equilibrio.

1.

Opening the door the trembling beast
—when I return
I will wrap myself in ferns
and turn the air bloody and lymph.
The tiresome skin will have dissolved
when the beast opens the door.

I rise up in the dream and repeat it, without will,
as it was in the stillness of the stone.

The wave departs from the eye, from the open land
—I spew lewd whispers.

Voice is the shadow, is the body.
Reason, point of light,
falls collapsed the tree of harmony.

2.

Pensamiento reducido a cenizas—
en el cielo dorado traza líneas.
Ya nada del tiempo, ya vacío.
Lo que impregna el aire es la duración de los follajes.

A la luz el que habla se hace clarividente
en las palabras casuales.
A la luz las escenas visibles ilustran lo invisible
para ojos no humanos.

Última noche.
Ni ruido ni imagen.
En la espera sin conciencia
el cuerpo se abandona.
A la inmensidad de océanos terrestres se abandona.

2.

Thought reduced to ashes—
tracing lines in the golden sky.
No more of time, already empty.
What soaks the air is the duration of the leaves.

In the light he who speaks turns clairvoyant
in an offhand remark.
In the light the visible scenes illuminate the unseeable
for inhuman eyes.

Final night.
Neither sound nor image.
In its unconscious waiting
the body surrenders.
To the expanse of earthly seas it surrenders.

3.

En otro lado dejaremos de sentir
impresiones que permanecerán en la boca de la cueva,
a saber: la habitación de los jardines,
el pulso de la marea.

Encontraré objetos de la noche —dije—
no esenciales al ojo animal,
porque he sido tigre-ángel
olvidando la visita del maestro.
Lo que iba a decir era una mirada muerta
o una cárcel de paredes crecientes.

El equilibrio es el que duerme, el despacioso.
Lo que empieza y no acaba
o está por suceder, desata la noche.

Abrázame, estrella—
no hay, en realidad, cadáver:
el vacío fue llenado
por error en huesos blancos.

3.

Elsewhere we will cease to feel
the impressions that remain in the mouth of the cave,
namely: the gardens' room,
the pulse of the tide.

I will find the night objects—I said—
unneeded by the animal eye,
because I've been tiger-angel
forgetting the teacher's visit.
What I'd wanted to say was a dead glance
or a prison of growing walls.

Harmony is the sleeper, the slow one.
What starts and doesn't finish
or is coming now, untying the night.

Embrace me, star—
there is truly no corpse:
the emptiness in white bones
was filled by mistake.

4.

He perdido el olvido de la muerte,
madre hechicera, separada de la herencia
excluyo las sombras.

Entro en el agua por la savia
que no toca la tierra.
Entro en el agua para concebir sin sexo
un cuerpo
y cada parte se ata a otra
sin lazos de sangre.

Animal salvaje
—la ceremonia es estéril.
Sobre flores amarillas
deposito el nacimiento.
Estallan los átomos en los espejos,
rostro y piel se desgarran.
En ese tiempo, qué es la eternidad,
qué es ojo, agujero, grito.

4.

I've lost the oblivion of death,
bewitching mother, divested of the inheritance
save for the shadows.

I enter the water through the sap
that doesn't touch the earth.
I enter the water to conceive immaculately
a body
and each part ties itself to another
without ropes of blood.

Savage animal
—the ceremony is sterile.
On a bed of yellow flowers
I deposit the birth.
The atoms in the mirrors burst,
face and skin rip apart.
In that moment, what is eternity,
what is sight, hole, scream.

5.

Soy yo ese aliento, brazos líquidos.
Respiro pegada a sábanas luminosas,
órbita o nube, aún más allá.

Soy yo la que huye
hacia estanques de materia.
Esa cuenca de las voces,
cueva virgen entre árboles de plumas
guarda todavía los dientes del río.

Un día cambia el tiempo.
La tierra cambia el tiempo.

Soy la que sueña,
quiero ser lo soñado.

5.

I am that breath, those fluid arms.
I breathe stuck to shining sheets,
orbit or cloud, even farther on.

I am the woman who flees
into material ponds.
That basin of voices,
the virgin cave amid feathered trees
still guards the river's teeth.

A day shifts time.
The earth shifts time.

I am the dreaming woman,
I want to be the dream.

6.

Yo soy —o era,
como una raíz desde lo lejos, desde siempre,
memoria en la carne, tan frágil.

De otra manera, poco a poco,
bajo distinta luz, la materia me hizo un rostro
y éste de ahora se vuelve mi muro.

Diré palabras que equivalgan al aire
asidas a la beatitud o la desesperación
—ese sol no se cierra con mis ojos.

Como en una gruta y el cielo de silencio
entrar de tu vientre nocturno a la ceguera,
traspasar el agua obedeciendo a la forma.
Construir de otra manera:
día a día, lentamente,
sobre puertas o piedras.

Yo soy —o era
eternamente, no-nada, diferencia.

6.

I am—or I was,
like a distant root, always there,
memory in the so fragile flesh.

In another way, little by little,
under a certain light, matter makes a face for me
and from now on this becomes my wall.

I'll offer words, weightless as air
attached to blessedness or despair
—that sun won't set with my eyes.

As if in a cavern and its silent heaven
to enter blindness from your nocturnal womb,
to pass through water obeying its form.
To build another way:
day by day, slowly,
over doors or stones.

I am—or I was
eternally, not-nothing, difference.

7.

Crecen los enigmas en el fluido de la noche
—se vierten en el agua helada
por una savia restituida que entra en las ramas,
en los rastros de las flores, hacia oscuros pinos.

Nombres, nombres —se cumplen los sueños
cuando el deseo es absoluto.
Un día entre animales, entre hojas
—dirijo la voz hacia el abismo.

Y el cuerpo del mar se amansa en el verano.
La adivinación de los templos silenciosos
es la sangre del mar.
El mar se aquieta en la memoria.
Nombres, nombres —se cumplen los sueños
cuando el deseo conoce el absoluto.

7.

Enigmas grow in the fluid of the night
—they're emptied into the frozen water
by a restored sap that enters the branches,
the traces of flowers, even darker pines.

Names, names—they complete the dreams
when desire is absolute.
A day among animals and leaves
—I direct my voice to the depths.

And the body of the sea soothes itself in summer.
The divination of silent temples
is the blood of the sea.
The sea quiets in memory.
Names, names—they complete the dreams
when desire meets the absolute.

8.

¿Miraremos desde nuestra trampa a los escarabajos?
¿los túneles de la hormiga? ¿el nido de los pájaros?
—Consumados destreza y saber en la fisura de lo salvaje.
Y en otros recovecos, algo como un tejido hambriento:
el agua y el aire, discontinuos, pueden trasvasarse.

Hubo un tiempo en que el espacio recibía el poder de una fuerza,
semejante a un pozo para atraer agujas.
—ahora el centro se aleja del ojo,
el ombligo del mundo parece ocultarse
y no nos es dado ver u oír la tierra.

Está también la madera que, según el shinto, debe ser destruida
a causa del halo formado por manos invisibles y vacías
—un hombre es un espacio, eslabón de lazos,
mientras la reverencia a la posesión pueda derribarse.
Hasta la Casa de Té dura una estación.

Pero Roma construye con piedras
destinadas a la eternidad de la ruina,
y en el tacto de mármoles y dulces curvas estatuarias
también el viaje a la muerte se enmascara:
dar aún un hilo a la parca.

8.

From our trap, will we watch the beetles?
The ant's tunnels? The birds' nests?
—consummate skill and wisdom in the fissures of the wild.
And in other nooks, something like a starving cloth:
water and air, disconnected, can decant themselves.

There was a time when space was granted a power,
like a well that attracts a needle
—now the center flees the eye,
the navel of the world seems to hide itself
and we can neither hear nor see the earth.

And in Shinto, the wood which carries the halo
of invisible, empty hands should be destroyed
—man is a space, a chain of knots
while the worship of possession can collapse.
Even the tea house lasts for a season.

But Rome built with stones
destined for ruin's eternity
and in the touch of marble and tender, stately curves
the voyage toward death is also disguised:
to offer still a thread to the Fates.

9.

Mistificación. Era esa la palabra,
la no abolida aún en el necesario contraste
del ser en el aparecer,
donde había arrojo en el miedo,
dolor en mi risa de alarde.

Aquella tarde se consteló el cielo
de nubes fantasmales
bajo el apoyo de una seda carnal
—contemplar era posible
como oír esa música
ablandada en una armonía aérea:
el sueño sin desplazamientos.

Entonces, la contemplación me reflejó
suspendida en un sorbo de tu lengua.
Podía ir y venir sobre las hebras del día,
comenzar el despliegue nocturno,
dar órdenes al mar.

Dependeré de ese residuo,
de lo que la uña raspa,
como un árbol rehecho en el silencio de raíces sucesivas,
royendo en la aridez, donde extravío
palabras sin memoria, la memoria de tus ojos.

9.

Mystification. That was the word,
not even abolished by the necessary contrast
of being in appearance,
where there was courage in fear,
pain in my showy laugh.

The sky constellated itself that afternoon
in phantasmal clouds
held up by an earthly silk
—thinking was possible
like hearing music
weakened in an airy harmony:
the dream without displacement.

Then, thinking reflected me
suspended in a mouthful of your language.
I could come and go amid the day's threads,
start the nightly unfolding,
give orders to the sea.

I will depend on that residue,
on what the nail scrapes,
like a tree recast in the silence of future roots,
gnawing in the dryness, where I misplace
words without memory, the memory of your eyes.

Sólo el ojo ve el azul

Only the Eye Sees Blue

1.

Sobre ese océano de azul pensante,
la lenta marea de flores a la deriva
tramadas de moho marino
cae en la porcelana de mantos de mortajas
a la luz, a la sombra declinante.

Sobre ese mar que se expande en el azul
de su cielo en ascenso, la trampa voluble
de los motivos de la meditación
como hilos frágiles en redes,
mientras el tiempo inmóvil sumerge afinados dedos
en los golpes de las olas
y las olas se rasgan como telas en el aire.

Por deseo fluye el agua
y de sus cristales, valvas y erizos
se destrozan inhumanos,
convertidos en ojos, pesada carne.

Sólo en el vaivén
el encantamiento del vacío.

1.

Over that ocean of thinking blue,
the slow tide of drifting flowers
woven of marine mold
falls in the chinaware of cloaks of shrouds
in the light, in the fading shadow.

Over that sea which expands in the blue
of its rising sky, the fickle trap
of meditation's motives
like webs of fragile threads,
while unmoving time sinks polished fingers
in the waves' blows
and the waves rip like fabric in the air.

Water flows driven by desire
and from its crystals, inhuman shells
and urchins shatter,
becoming eyes, heavy flesh.

Alone in the swaying,
the enchantment of the void.

2.

La tijera corta el agua, el cordón invisible
y vibra la mañana invernal, cerrándose
en cristales —en verdad su vientre es esa bolsa
atada a los tallos, a la flor
repetida, implícita.
Su vientre no es una boca,
se ha cerrado a la siesta
indagando en el equilibrio.

En silencio imposible los sauces me balancean
mientras se corta el agua iluminada por tu ojo
—me pierdo deseando entrar en tu sangre,
me pierdo llevando mi cuerpo al viento.

2.

Shears slice the water, the invisible cord
and the wintry morning vibrates, closing itself
in crystals—truly its womb is the pouch
tethered to the stalks, to the repeated,
implied flower.
Its womb is no mouth,
it has closed itself to the repose
investigating harmony.

In impossible silence the willows balance me
while the water splits illuminated by your eye.
—I lose myself wanting to enter your blood,
I lose myself lifting my body to the wind.

3.

La niebla atravesó el cielo, tendió un aliento de sombras sobre los vidrios
como preludio de paredes más espesas que el moho.

Ese junio cayó por orden de una máquina invisible
en oleadas grisáceas.

Los colores que eran las llamas se apagaban
en el frío —sólo el aire frío.
Objetos pasajeros flotaban tras la ventanilla.

Sobre la línea de los muros
ramas como agujas nacían a la luz lunar.
La desnudez de los árboles en ese mar de nubes
empezó a dibujar mi espacio.
—Mi espacio y yo éramos un ojo de dolor.

3.

The fog crossed the sky, stretching a shadowy breath against the
    windowpanes
as a prelude to walls thicker than mold.

That June fell by order of a machine invisible
in grayish waves.

The colors that comprised the flames extinguished
in the cold—just the cold air.
Fleeting objects floated past the little window.

Above the wall line
branches like needles were born in the moonlight.
The nakedness of the trees in that sea of clouds
began to mark my space.
—My space and I were an eye of pain.

4.

Semilla en el paisaje—
ni siquiera lo cruel agrieta el espejo geométrico.

Miramos lentamente las formas, figuras ahí aparecidas,
y amanece y anochece—
pero la pasividad, vidrio lunar,
sólo separa lo horizontal del cielo.

Luz ambigua late en los peces verdes,
en las aguas verdes,
 ¿qué señal se moverá?

En el fondo de la garganta
siento que me separo del mundo
porque el aire es la médula abierta.

Ríos helados corren y tiemblan
mientas la luz late en los peces verdes,
en las aguas verdes
como hojas de árboles soñados.

4.

Seed in the landscape—
not even the cruel cracks the geometric mirror.

Slowly we watch the forms, figures there appearing,
and the sun rises and sets—
but indifference, lunar glass,
only separates the horizontal from the sky.

Ambiguous light lurks in green fish,
in green waters,
which sign will stir?

In the depths of my throat,
I feel myself separate from the world
because the air is open marrow.

Frozen rivers flow and tremble
while light lurks in the green fish,
in the green waters
like leaves of the trees of dreams.

5.

La visión del día se disuelve
y se convierte en un rostro que mira.
El reloj marca la palpitación
que el cuerpo imprime.

Qué era pensar —verde en la sombra,
verde en la costra que cubre la montaña.
Frutas salinas aparecen desde el agua
desmenuzadas por tu mano.

Para no despertar sobrenado en la pasión
que sólo el ojo-dios conoce.
El mal ha muerto pero su red sostiene
un cielo de dardos.

Juntas las palabras inertes para recomenzar,
para atravesar la quietud a contraluz
—caja de mármol rosado.
Qué esperar —el gozo es el desasosiego.

5.

The day's vision dissolves
and becomes a peering face.
The watch marks the beat
that the body imposes.

What was it to think—green in the shadow,
green in the crust that covers the mountain.
Salty fruits emerge from the water
shredded by your hand.

So as not to wake I float on the passion
that only the god-eye knows.
Evil has died but its web sustains
a heaven of darts.

You join lifeless words to start over,
to traverse the backlit calm
—box of pink marble.
What was hope—pleasure is unease.

6.

atravesar el cuerpo del verano
—cada forma colmada y cada sentido
absorbiendo ese esplendor maduro, extenso

allí ese aire en la quietud de la mañana
ardor hasta las cenizas
una parte roja o dorada —el color cautivo
en la sucesión de lo visible

en la quietud de la mañana
la memoria hace audible lo animal
—la roca quebrada sobre la tierra abierta
y el follaje apenas azulado
no como adorno, no como máscara

otro vuelo busca de nuevo lo celeste
alrededor del cuerpo del verano,
dice el éxtasis de la caída
—evadir la metáfora pensada en la atalaya
abandonar la idea como se abandona el tiempo

6.

to pierce the summer's body
—each form brimming and each sense
absorbing this ripe, extensive splendor.

there that air in the stillness of morning
burning to ashes
a red or golden part—the color caught
in the sequence of the visible

in the stillness of morning
memory makes the animal audible
—the rock broken above the open earth
and the foliage barely bluish
not like adornment, not like a mask.

around the summer's body, another flight searches
again for the heavenly,
tells the ecstasy of the fall
—to avoid the metaphor formed in the watchtower
to abandon the notion as time is abandoned

7.

La noche consiste en la luz,
la forma fría de la piedra.

La palabra reemplaza a la mañana,
pero: no pensar la mañana
—la que llega a mí se deshace
y no puede comenzar, se consuma en la deriva.
Todo lugar es extranjero.

La noche del sueño se acerca sin imagen,
replica a los sentidos:
vuelco los objetos, desciendo, desaparezco.

Espero ante todo la sustitución del deseo
—que la naturaleza entre en el cuerpo
bajo pliegues amorfos, hable a la memoria.

¿Qué separa los imposibles
de esos restos que la razón hizo ver:
alas en la cabeza del lobo, garras en el pez?

7.

Night is composed of light,
the cold form of rock.

The word replaces the morning,
but: don't think of the morning
—she who comes to me dissolves
and can't begin, consumed by the tide.
Every place is foreign.

The night of dreams nears without image,
answering the senses:
I overturn objects, descending, disappearing.

I wish most of all to replace desire
—that nature would enter the body
under formless folds, speak to memory.

What divides the impossible
from those remainders that reason reveals:
wings on the skull of the wolf, the fish's claws?

El conocimiento siembra el cuerpo

Knowledge Scatters the Body

1.

Una voz como una puerta, como el aliento,
tu fuerza como una noche, como otra noche.

La mente se abre hacia ese canto mitad inferno
—un mundo exacto o vago, el tiempo abandonado.

Decía, leía, repetición de lo visible,
sorda al temor, ciega al misterio.

Recomienzo las pausas que habitan el sol
porque ese momento duplica tu tierra secreta.

Qué gracia incompleta —aun como personas
aparecemos en la vestidura de goce de la piel.

Quemamos piedras para tu alabanza
en el ojo vacío del invierno.

Y ese olvido que extiende las palabras
rescata atributos en las veces del dolor.

Nada exterior tiene pies o raíces
—es esa hora que sucede o se aniquila
hacía la saciedad, la certidumbre.

1.

A voice like a door, like breath,
your strength like a night, like another night.

The mind opens toward that half-hellish song
—a world exact or vague, time abandoned.

I spoke, I read, repetition of the visible,
deaf to fear, blind to mystery.

I take up the pauses that dwell in the sun
because those moments mimic your secret lands.

What incomplete grace—even like people
we appear in the pleasing vestments of skin.

We burn rocks in your praise
in the empty eye of winter.

And the oblivion from which words spread
rescues symbols in times of pain.

Nothing outside has roots or feet
—it's that hour that occurs or dissolves
into satiety, certainty.

2.

Quise llamar desde el aire a tu imagen
—hermano de la estrella es tu nombre.

Hasta la muerte —pensé—
y era insípido beber poseyendo sólo los desechos.

Desde esa montaña negra que cubre tu llama,
hasta la muerte —pensé—
iría atravesando piedras,
el tiempo destruiría la arena,
la noche árida sería el primer bosque.

El agua que desaparecía destinada a la costumbre
respondía en mí como palabra fría
para recorrer un cuerpo ya extrañado.

Quise llamar, pero aquí yazgo
bajo las infinitas alas de la noche.

2.

I wanted to call through the air to your image
—brother of the star is your name.

Until death—I thought—
and it was tedious, having only the dregs to drink.

From that black mountain that conceals your flame,
until death—I thought—
I would go crossing stones,
time would abolish the dunes,
the arid night would be the first forest.

The water that vanished according to custom
answered in me like a cold word
to course through a body already shocked.

I wanted to call, but here I lie,
under the infinite wings of night.

3.

La travesía es el tiempo.
La travesía es la mutación.
Acuarios hechos con rocío o lágrimas
y el viento sobre los pies
en el sentido de los gusanos.

Mascas como un lobo la luz
y dejas aparte el fruto del verano,
casi rencor abierto —el cuchillo hace de espejo
y divide el juego, del limbo.

Ahora amor en la boca impotente,
la eternidad despoblada —vacío, vacío.
Perder la palabra es el comienzo
para perder la verdad—
pero no sangras porque no existe.

Es el comienzo sobre la pirca nocturna:
traspasar la risa a la bestia,
la semejanza a otra semejanza.

3.

Time is the journey.
Change is the journey.
Aquariums filled with dew or tears
and the wind over your feet
as worms would be.

You chew light like a wolf,
and leave the summer fruit aside,
almost in open rancor—the knife is a mirror
dividing the game from limbo.

Now love in the impotent mouth,
the deserted eternity—empty, empty.
To lose the word is the first step
to losing truth—
but you don't bleed because it doesn't exist.

It's the first step over the stony wall of night:
to cross from the smile to the beast
from likeness to another likeness.

4.

Cómo vivir —extravío ese centelleo
donde se anuncia la huida provisoria
y traspasa la médula metálica.

Para vencer el umbral coloco en la lengua
la hostia y dejo que me atraviese.

El vaticinio resuena en la voz
y se expande hacia la piel, la pureza del ojo
elevándose en rayos —a dios esperará.

Cómo vivir, digo,
a la pálida luz de los abismos
donde nombre y objeto no aceptan compararse.

4.

How to live—I lose that spark
where the conditional escape is declared
and pierce the metallic medulla.
To cross the threshold I place the host
on my tongue and let it pass through me.

The prophecy echoes in the voice
and spreads to the skin, the purity of the eye
rising in light—it will wait for god.

How to live, I say,
in the pallid light of the chasms
where name and thing permit no compare.

5.

La mutación se sucede como las sombras,
esa montaña parece sangrar en el comienzo de la noche.

Hablo en lo transitorio, busco en lo transitorio
y las señas pasan por el silencio de las cicatrices.

Después del mar, la tierra.
Después de la tierra, los ojos
—placer maternal.

En todas partes derramas las preguntas
que se alinean en el mapa de la sed.
Sin guía tus pasos me encuentran
y aun sin fruta tu boca es mordida.
Ahora mis brazos se alargan
para llegar a tu carne desnuda.

Y en el pensamiento tu semejanza ms sostiene
para huir del temor o del éxtasis.

5.

Change follows like the shadows,
as night falls that mountain seems to bleed.

I speak in the provisional, I search in the provisional
and the signs pass through the silence of scars.

After the sea, the land.
After the land, the eyes
—maternal pleasure.

You spill questions everywhere
which arrange themselves on thirst's map.
Guideless your steps find me
and even without fruit your mouth is worn.
Now my arms stretch
to arrive at your naked flesh.

And in thinking your likeness sustains me
to flee from terror or ecstasy.

6.

Donde excava, cae, se resbala, cae.
Acaso también la tierra sostenga su ceniza.
Una raíz engendra su boca
—la hendidura por donde la luz vuelve,
al fin, no sensible, no sensitiva.

Allí vacilo —andén de espera.
La desnudez sólo en el cuerpo,
en la piel de los bordes.
El vértigo para no sentir, apenas un instante.

Contigua al sueño, la noche
como mera vanidad
se abre en la pendiente.
Y excava, cae, se resbala, cae.

Ese punto fondo, roca, soga.
Ese punto vacío, error de eternidad,
simula la última gracia:
es mundo inesperado para pasajeros quietos
—la elisión de la carne,
mientras una parte del deseo cae, se resbala, cae.

6.

Where it digs, falls, slips and falls.
Maybe the earth too will hold its ashes.
A root conceives its mouth
—the crack where the light returns
in the end, not sensitive, not sensory.

There I stagger—the waiting platform.
Nudity alone in the body,
in the skin of the borders.
The frenzy not to feel, just for an instant.

Adjoining the dream, the night
like mere vanity
cracks open on the slope.
And it digs, falls, slips and falls.

That bottom point, rock, noose.
That empty point, error of eternity,
simulates the ultimate grace:
the unexpected world for motionless travelers
—the body's elision,
while a part of desire falls, slips, and falls.

7.

No he despertado aún—
ignoro la controversia del cuerpo,
la que relaciona los ojos al dolor
y de esa puerta todo el tiempo
emana el comienzo de las cosas
—falsos órganos de flores iniciales.

No he despertado aún.
Me hundo día a día en las palabras solares,
la aspereza equívoca de las playas de luz.

Lejos de la conciencia
querré decir lo ausente del recuerdo
—algo monstruoso o verdadero.

Lo que cambia en la corriente
está atado al agua
—destruye en tu boca parásitos,
hojas dentadas sobre lianas de hiel.

Pero la seda del ojo en desequilibrio
ya no puede observar.
Esclavitud ambigua
—hacer de lo verbal lo interior.

7.

Still I have not awakened—
I ignore the body's controversy,
which links eyes to pain
and from that doorway always
emanate the beginnings of things
—false organs of the first flowers.

Still I have not awakened.
Day by day I sink in solar words,
the misunderstood roughness of the beaches of light.

Far from conscience
I'll want to say what's absent from memory
—something monstrous or true.

What changes in the current
is tied to water
—destroying parasites in your mouth,
jagged leaves over vines of bile.

But the unbalanced silk of the eye
can no longer observe.
Ambiguous bondage
—to make the spoken come inside.

8.

El impulso del mar, vacío en la repetición
y las horas, convergiendo como un vuelo.

Bañarse en las orillas, para hacer aparecer
la desnudez en oposición a las nubes.

Equivoco el sueño, el rocío—
a lo largo de esa distancia desfigurada
se borra el hueco de las puertas.

Sale y entra el cuerpo.
Todo el horizonte espera el sobresalto de las piedras.

Y sobre la sangre se deslizan besos,
de tus labios, besos.

La trampa del tiempo.
Es inmóvil ahora.

Y cae en el cuerpo inmóvil, la mirada inmóvil.
La luz en los espejos se hace oblicua
y se clava en el viento.

El tiempo atraviesa extremidades,
se pliega a la necesidad de la piel.

8.

The thrust of the sea, empty in its repetition
and the hours, converging like a flight.

To bathe on the shore, so that nakedness
appears in opposition to the clouds.

I confuse the dream, the dew—
across that distorted distance
the space between the doors fades.

The body exits and enters.
The horizon awaits the shock of the stones.

And kisses glide on the blood,
from your lips, kisses.

The trap of time.
It's motionless now.

And it falls into the motionless body, the motionless glance.
The light in the mirrors turns oblique
and is pinned to the wind.

Time pierces limbs,
submitting to the necessity of skin.

9.

Con tu saliva olvido los pies de la noche
—los que llevan al tiempo o al hastío.

Todavía es remoto el lugar donde podría estar.
Encuentro nombres para el yo
y no otro —impotencia de emerger
hacia la estela del agua, las sombras
de las sombras, lo que hace navegar y no acaba.

Día sin fin —no puede cambiarse
por tiempo en mí,
ni aniquilar sobre la finitud
los cielos del sentido.

Con tu saliva quiebro la razón,
entro en espacios de anémonas.
Seré nada en el aire, eco en las voces
—la presencia en el encantamiento
como placer carnal, como certeza.

9.

With your spit I forget the night's stride
—what leads to time or boredom.

The place where I could be is distant still.
I find names for myself
and no other—the helplessness of surfacing
toward the water's trail, the shadows
of the shadows, what makes you sail without end.

Unending day—it can't be exchanged
for the time in me,
nor annihilate the skies
of sense over finitude.

With your spit I fracture reason,
I enter anemone spaces.
I will be nothing in the air, an echo in the voices
—the presence in the spell
like a carnal pleasure, like certainty.

Diario

Diary

1.

Necesidad del día. Incidencia de las horas en el único rayo. La ansiedad de lo que se espera es fugaz. Lechosa y rosada luz de los amaneceres húmedos —todo parece ahora distante.

1.

The necessity of the day. The event of the hours in the singular ray.
The anxiety of what's expected is fleeting. Creamy, pink light of humid dawns—it all seems distant now.

2.

El sol de enero impregna el aire con ardor árido.
Quiero recomenzar. Es un ejercicio de abstención —el desarrollo de la sensibilidad del aire.
"la canción de los pinos" —nombra Darío.

2.

The January sun impregnates the air with arid ardor.
I want to start over. It's an exercise of abstention—to develop
the sensibility of the air.
"the song of the pines"—as Darío says.

3.

Días en que el sol abre un manto grave, denso. Y la lluvia imaginada es como una lámina de hojalata.
Todavía, francotirador de los domingos, me lanzo al chillido de los pájaros.
Hierba rala.
Me embriago con la luna, con los nombres de las quejas.
Cae el silencio: mi montaña, mi torre.

3.

Days when the sun opens a dense, somber cloak. And the imaginary rain is like a sheet of tinplate.
Still, sniper of Sundays, I launch myself into the cries of the birds.
Thinning grass.
I'm drunk on the moon, on the names of grievances.
Silence falls: my mountain, my tower.

4.

Es la tarde la que es eterna, la que desposita la melancolía sobre los párpados, la que me hunde en esta marea de espacios. El punto relativo es el velo del dolor. No puedo caminar más que entre árboles.
¿Eres nueva en el puente invisible? —dicen.
Transfórmame, amado mío, haz que crezca en lo perecedero, en la muerte de mi infancia.

4.

It's the afternoon which is eternal, which places melancholy over my eyelids, sinking me into this tide of spaces.
The relative point is the veil of pain. I cannot walk anymore save between trees.
"Are you new to the invisible bridge?" they say.
Transform me, my love, make me grow in the perishable, in the death of my infancy.

5.

La forma es la lunación.
Respiro el olvido a través de tu ojo azul.

5.

The lunar cycle is the form.
I breathe oblivion through your blue eye.

6.

Vueltas y vueltas. Ilusión demencial y el miedo al extravío.
No descanso porque los dones tienen máscaras. Me sostiene el azar.

Me desvío en el vértigo, en las letras sospechosas.
Esa luz grisácea hace llorar, descender.
Y descendiendo me aparto del sueño, de los pliegues de la pasión.

Promesa de no resistir, de no sumergirme en el líquido de la espera.

6.

Turning and turning. A crazy illusion and the fear of loss.
I don't rest because the gifts have masks. I'm kept aloft by fate.

I break away in the vertigo, in the suspicious letters.
That grayish light makes me cry and descend.
And descending, I turn from the dream, from the folds of passion.

A promise not to resist, not to submerge myself in the waters of delay.

7.

Miro a mi alrededor y veo la subyugación del vacío —y a veces sólo eso. Este paseo sobre las pequeñas cosas, su suspensión, como la seducción del abismo, no allanan los primeros obstáculos. ¿Necesidad de un maestro? Derrumbe silencioso. Descender a ese abismo —el de las sucesivas caídas, el del futuro desligado del tiempo, como río de los posibles.

7.

I look around and see the subjugation of emptiness—and sometimes, nothing more.
This pass above the small things, their suspension, like the seduction of the abyss, can't flatten the primary obstacles. Is a teacher needed?
Silent collapse. To descend to that abyss—of successive falls, of a future unhitched from time, like a river of the possible.

8.

El goce es una franja inhumana en el cuerpo, trozo ingrávido. La roca es una divinidad en el viento, la pureza de un día por venir —que aparta la muerte con un gesto impotente.

Nacer, en verdad, nacer, en la constelación de los errantes, de los fugitivos —probar diminutos frutos, callejas desconocidas.

8.

Pleasure is an inhuman band on the body, a weightless piece. The stone is a divinity in the wind, the purity of a coming day—which sets aside death with an impotent gesture.

To be born, to be truly born, under the sign of wanderers, of fugitives—to try the diminutive fruits, the unknown alleys.

9.

El verano agobia con la certeza de la movilidad, de que el goce, al detener el tiempo, nos convierte en huidizas aves. Se anula lo humano. Prudencia de los árboles —sus vibraciones complacen el silencio, lo entremezclan de lianas solares.

9.

Summer oppresses with the certainty of movement, such that pleasure, to slow time, turns us to elusive birds.
The human is annulled. The prudence of the trees—their vibrations please the silence, mixing it with solar vines.

10.

El verano complace una parte del deseo del cuerpo —pero ese deseo no estaría sin la luz de ojos en la edificación de los objetos. Objetos lacustres, tapiz terreno, espejos. No puedo unir partes ni átomos, ni brazos. Atolladero carnal —con el peso de los días suplantar la fuerza de los montes, la atrofia de la dicha. Salvaje caducidad, inmóvil.

10.

Summer pleases a part of the body's desire—desire that wouldn't exist without the light of eyes on the construction of objects. Lakeside objects, earthy tapestry, mirrors. I can unite neither parts nor atoms, nor arms. A carnal mire—with the weight of the days supplanting the force of the hills, the atrophy of speech.

A savage expiration, unmoving.

11.

Me duermo sobre esta tierra acre.
Quejas —un túmulo de ruinas de las que surge la "boca de la esfinge."
Sombras en el borde del mar, mientras me duermo.

Imposibilidad de soportar la debilidad de las puertas.

11.

I sleep atop this acrid land.
Grievances—a barrow of ruins from which the "mouth of the Sphinx" arises.
Shadows on the border of the sea, while I sleep.

The impossibility of bearing the weakness of the doors.

12.

Se revuelcan en el barro hojas y ramas, y crecen árboles sobre el silencio —ese silencio es el sitio humano desgarrado en selvas de callado mirar, en agujeros.
Placer en el país del aire.

12.

Leaves and branches wallow in the mud, and trees grow atop the silence—that silence is the torn human space in forests of quiet watching, in holes.
Pleasure in the nation of air.

13.

No puedo adaptarme al comienzo —y eso, en realidad, sólo al comienzo. El futuro es como un hueco, al que se tiene la ilusión de llenar. ¿Pero qué es, sino el descenso hacia el fin de nuestros días, el hundimiento en ese espacio difuso, en ese tiempo difuso, en que no seremos? La palabra de la finitud es un alimento de gestos aparentes, de sueños frágiles. La experiencia de la finitud nos libera de la posesión, de la distancia, de la idea de la continuidad, de los alcances del dolor.

No puedo adaptarme al comienzo. Y vuelvo a comenzar. Y vuelvo a comenzar. ¿Qué ha cambiado en el transcurso de estas horas, de estos días, de estos años? Pierdo lo vago del olvido y bebo en la ansiedad.

El sol de raíces verticales, la fatalidad de cristales de imán.

13.

I cannot adapt to the beginning—and in fact, only to the beginning. The future is like a hole, one that has the illusion of being filled. But what is it, other than a descent to the end of our days, the sinking into that diffuse space, that diffuse time, in which we will not be?
To speak of the finite is a nourishment of obvious gestures, of fragile dreams. The experience of the finite frees us from possession, from distance, from the idea of continuity, from the reaches of pain.

I cannot adapt to the beginning. And I begin again. And I begin again. What has changed in the span of these hours, these days, these years? I lose the vagueness of oblivion and drink down anxiety.
Sun of vertical roots, the doom of the magnet's crystals.

14.

Viaje entre árboles —formas diversas, follajes silenciosos. El verano es silencioso en la aridez, en la ausencia de ese viento que agita, provoca a lo estático como espera.

En medio de follajes sin olor —necesidad de humedad para que el olor se expanda, sobre el suelo y el aire.

Aridez del verano, quietud. La vibración de los colores sacude los objetos. La ciudad se hace misteriosa, mecánica.

14.

To travel through trees—diverse forms, silent leaves.
Summer is silent in its dryness, in the absence of that agitating wind which, like waiting, provokes the ecstatic.
Surrounded by scentless leaves—the necessity of humidity for the scent to expand, above the earth and air.
Dryness of summer, quietude. The vibration of the colors shakes the objects. The city turns mysterious, mechanical.

15.

Por un ojo-de-artificio es posible percibir la detención del tiempo. En el verano el tiempo se detiene —y se hace diáfano, y se abandona a la expansión de los cuerpos. Ellos están y no existen, borran la conciencia de sí, borran la idea —no es sólo ese placer, no es sólo su persistencia.
¿Qué es lo que coincide con la palabra?
Este verano es una pared de espejos.

15.

With an artificial eye, it's possible to see the stoppage of time.
In summer, time stops, turns diaphanous, abandons itself to the expansion of bodies. They are and they don't exist, they erase the consciousness of themselves, they erase the idea—it's not only that pleasure, it's not only its persistence.
What coincides with the word?
This summer is a wall of mirrors.

16.

Arriesgo, errando, mi propio límite.
El riesgo es un extravío. Si puedo errar en el silencio, me situaré a tu lado, podré ser esa frase olvidada, la que se pierde, vivir en el centelleo de las edificaciones sin infinito.

16.

Wandering, I risk my own limit.
The risk is a loss. If I can wander in the silence, I'll find myself at your side, I'll become that forgotten phrase, the missing one, living in the sparkling of buildings without infinity.

17.

¿Qué es lo que recomienza? La escritura, deambulando sobre deseos urdidos en escombros de otros deseos, ahora lejanos. Recomienzo la escritura —su placer anárquico, agradable, inflexible en su exigencia. Y al recomenzar me alejo del cumplimiento de esa construcción sobre el cuerpo, que se diluye en sus cortezas.

Profusión de mínimas acciones, rayos —sin mansedumbre atacan, atraviesan con sus astas negras los aspectos aislados en los sentidos. Lo sensible refugia frutos salvajes (¿tal vez mezquinos?) de cada instante inmediato, o de la inmediatez de los instantes percibidos en medio de gestos, de acciones, no vacíos ni nimios —despojados incluso de lo caduco.

17.

What is it that begins again? Writing, wandering among warped desires in the ruins of other desires, distant now. I take up writing again—its anarchic joy, pleasing and inflexible in its demands. And in starting anew I drift away from the completion of that structure above the body, which is dissolved in its shell.

A profusion of minor actions, rays of light—without gentleness they attack, with their black horns they traverse the isolated aspects of the senses. The sensible shelters the savage (or maybe miserly?) fruits of each immediate instant, or of the immediacy of the instants perceived amid gestures and actions, neither empty nor trivial—stripped even of the obsolete.

18.

¿Qué es lo que recomienzo? —la escritura, la escritura que pretende ser una lectura, tamizar con los signos la espesura del mundo. Y el mundo siempre se configura para sus fines, y la contemplación sólo se desarrolla en analogías.

La escritura como analogía —y no como expresión: construir otra naturaleza sin moral, sin biomas. Entonces eso: una experiencia de abstención y una construcción poética que exhiba su desarrollo como su símbolo, a la vez vacío de referente, vacío de explicaciones, aislado de ideas.

18.

What is it that I begin again? Writing, writing that seeks to be a reading, to sift with signs the thickness of the world. And the world always configures itself to its own ends, and thinking only develops in analogies.

Writing as an analogy—and not as expression: to construct another nature without morals, without biomes. Okay, then: an experience of abstention, a poetic construction which projects its development as its own symbol, at once empty of reference, empty of explications, isolated from ideas.

19.

Extravío. Vuelvo sobre el bosque y sobre la idea del bosque. Voy errando, con un sueño que se corta al amanecer, y en la noche se repite, como una tela celeste o astral —indivisa en sí, sin espesura.

19.

Loss. I return to the forest and the idea of the forest. I go wandering, with a dream that cuts off at dawn and at night begins anew, like an astral or heavenly thread—indivisible in itself, without presence.

20.

Acantonada en el estado en que nada puede determinar su terreno-territorio. Los elementos se superponen: lo concreto a lo sensible, lo nocturno a lo idéntico.

En el éxtasis, la refracción me muestra la simetría de cada gesto, de cada palabra: la simetría es el ritual vacío del arte, su trampa.

20.

Stationed in the state where nothing can determine its earth-territory. The elements superimpose themselves: the concrete onto the sensible, the nocturnal onto the identical. In ecstasy, the refraction shows me the symmetry of every gesture, of every word: symmetry is the empty ritual of art, its trap.

Otras poemas

Other Poems

Amor en océanos de arena

1.

el horizonte acostado sobre la piel de las piedras
a la edad de los caminos tu libertad o tu desnudez
el peso muerto de los brazos escucha las tormentas

pensamiento indefinido —brota sin razones desde una boca
(hubiera amado sin memoria en la tumba de la noche)

no llega jamás
adentro queda
en el cuerpo queda
no llega
no hay

hubiera amado —sed de todas las voces
mellando a fuego lento el cristal de los ojos
más fuerte la prueba de la certidumbre
dormita agazapada
al margen de los besos crecen puertas de melancolía

Love in Oceans of Sand

1.

the horizon draped over the skin of the rocks
as old as the roads your freedom or nakedness
the dead weight of the arms hears the storms

undefined thought—it sprouts without reasons from a mouth
(I would have loved without memory in the night's tomb)

never arrives
remains inside
remains in the body
doesn't arrive
doesn't exist

I would have loved—thirst of all voices
slowly eroding the crystal of the eyes
at higher heat the proof of certainty
sleeps huddled
at the edge of the kiss sprout doors of melancholy

2.

me alimento de lo que amo
devoro esa carne y sus huecos irreales
como en un océano amoroso
en el que nado sin pérdida
—sin pérdida de pasión ni del pulso de la sangre

los sentidos ya no pueden separarse—
leche del cielo bebo más y más
y en mi boca los pensamientos atraviesan el tiempo

para equilibrar el paisaje ahora bebo
leche del cielo, bebo más y más
y hago en mí la orilla vegetal que ocupas
para conservar la imagen de diferencia
—hálito es fuerza,
no aliento que recorre y penetra
sino hálito de exhalación

2.

I feed on what I love
devouring flesh and its unreal bones
as in a loving ocean
in which I swim without loss
—without loss of passion or the pulse

the senses can no longer be separated—
heavenly milk I drink more and more
and in my mouth thinking crosses time

to balance the landscape now I drink
heavenly milk, I drink more and more
and create in myself the vegetal shore where you stand
to maintain the image of difference
—breath is force
not spirit that crosses and enters
but the breath of exhalation

3.

bastaría la idea de persona
para perderse en sucesivas muertes

nada simple —a causa de los días
la orilla se desliza

ir y venir sobre tu lengua
y mares hechos de palabras
inconvenientes al sueño
o al escudo de los sueños

pruebo abrirte con el tacto y mi sangre
y la prueba se deshace

en el extremo giro
para volverme dócil a la sombra
y la desnudez muestra tu imagen

3.

the idea of a person suffices
to lose yourself in successive deaths

by no means easy—days cause
the shore to slide by

to come and go on your tongue
and seas made of words
unsuitable to the dream
or the shield of dreams

I try to open you with my tact and blood
and the evidence dissolves

I turn to the extreme
becoming docile again in the shadow
and nudity reveals your image

4.

Buscando centros opuestos
cambiaremos enteramente el cuerpo
—la plenitud se sella en los símbolos.

Temprano iré sobre el camino del mar:
una estrella también es un sitio
o la luna, cuando hace surgir sus reflejos
sobre los mapas nocturnos.
Daré rodeos hasta que haya terminado el día.

¿Qué idea podrá corresponderse con el deseo?
Depende de la nube, del canto del pájaro,
de la suposición de la voz.

Ese resto de razón se duplica
en la felpa de la arena, áspera e insípida,
y vuela sobre ti y te divide,
mientras habito dulcemente la noche.
Dos nunca son uno—
miente la reina que conjura el páramo.

4.

Searching for opposing centers
we will change the body entirely
—fullness is sealed in symbols.

Early I will travel the ocean's road:
a star too is a place
or the moon, when it makes its reflection appear
on the maps of night.
I'll detour until the end of day.

Which idea will correspond to desire?
It depends on the cloud, on the bird's song,
on the assumption of the voice.

What remains of reason doubles
in the plush of sand, rough and dull,
and circles you and divides you
while sweetly I inhabit the night.
Two are never one—
lies the queen who conjures the wasteland.

5.

En la oreja y en el cuello, tierno, ligero,
lo táctil de la amapola.
—Suscitar inquietud, ardor
¿no es eso lo que imaginamos?
Demasiadas líneas, brotes de los ríos
sobre el azul del agua de la pupila en huso.

La existencia empieza en ese amor
dominado en el tatuaje de las alas.
Abres tu beso —no eres.

No ya. Dirección del viento o el origen del viento.
Frutos únicos los buscados
sobre tus caminos, antes que las cicatrices
ahogaron estrellas
o esa ciudad-pez flameara en la memoria.

Lento fuego, tu caricia me recorre.
Nada perenne —contemplo a los muertos
desde sus propias palabras, sin la prisión de las lágrimas.

Y a lo largo pasan los pinos, pasan los cipreses.
Cerrada con plomo invento un tiempo.

5.

On the ear and the neck, tender, light,
the brush of the poppy.
—To provoke concern, ardor,
isn't this what we imagined?
Too many lines, sprouts of rivers
above the blue of the water of the spindled pupil.

Existence begins in that love
mastered by the tattoo of wings.
You open your kiss—you don't exist

No longer. Direction of the wind or the wind's origin.
Unique fruits those sought
on your paths, before the scars
drowned stars
or that fish-city burning in memory.

Slow fire, your caress runs through me.
By no means eternal—I study the dead
by their own words, without the jail of tears.

And eventually the pines pass, the cypresses pass.
Sealed with lead I invent a time.

6.

¿Era yo aquella a quien amabas?
Si retrocede la hora, permanece el polvo,
succiona cada cuerpo bajo la luna
el aire letal.

Canto mi pertenencia a la noche
y dejo caer los restos al agua.

En el atardecer, abrázame,
hunde tu lengua en mi vulva
porque he soñado que tocaba
la sustancia despojada de tu carne
—y mientras lo hacía
lo fugaz no era la voz sino la muerte.

Tiempo es estremecimiento.
¿Era yo aquella a quien amabas
si ya no es el lugar, ni la forma?
Los cuerpos se hacen líquidos en la risa de la oscuridad.

6.

Was I one you loved?
If the hour retreats, the dust remains,
beneath the moon each body absorbing
the lethal air.

I sing my belonging to the night
and let the rest fall to the water.

In dusk, embrace me,
sink your tongue into my vulva
because I have dreamed of touching
your essence stripped of flesh
—and when I did
it was death, not voice, that was fleeting.

Time is a tremor.
Was I one you loved
if this is no longer the place, nor the form?
Bodies turn fluid as darkness laughs.

Psique y eros

1.

Era antes, cuando se inclinaron, alma, tus efigies,
antes que una edad arrancara esmalte y barro,
y se descubriera la imagen: hombre-pájaro, cuerpo alado,
o las plumas del gallo oracular,
sin que fuera todavía insecto, fetiche hacia la mariposa
o la parábola de mujer-en-el-vuelo.

Después vino el rey que, oído el mandato, colocó tres estatuas en la maleza
—núbiles mejillas, muslos de cera.
El presagio de la madrépora ósea acechó a la elegida:
serpiente contra el himen, lento espectro en el cuello de la ventana.
Y cuando te llevaron, Psique, el cortejo era la mirada que vio tu muerte.
Pero tu pensamiento huyó de la roca donde eras la ofrenda,
y se convirtió en el ala negra del anhelo
—el temor alzó sus muros, paredes donde la memoria quebraría cristales.
Lo-por-venir veía una línea invisible en la entraña del árbol.

Psyche and Eros

    1.

It was earlier, soul, when your effigies bowed,
before an age would wrestle enamel and mud,
and discover the image: bird-man, winged body
or the feathers of an oracular rooster,
still without being insect, a fetish for the butterfly
or the parable of woman-in-flight.

Then came the king who, hearing the order, erected three statues in
    the weeds
—nubile cheeks, thighs of wax.
The bony madrepora's omen stalked the chosen one:
serpent against the hymen, a slow specter in the window's throat.
And when they woke you, Psyche, courtship was the vision that
    foresaw your death.
But your thinking fled the stone where you were the offering
and became the black wing of desire
—fear erected its barricade, walls where memory would shatter
    crystals.
What was yet to come saw an invisible line in the tree's guts.

2.

La prueba del desierto fue ese rapto, el relámpago que traslada hacia
   aguas de ceniza
—en el efímero jardín, raíces abre-puños, danzas de hojas
   confidentes,
húmedos, arbóreos techos, urdidos con los pétalos que se doblan en
   la casa del viento.
Eros tocó —en el embozo se hizo máscara de la noche,
el ausente de los infiernos.
Recorrió el tacto la suntuosidad
y el abrazo fue la rama infinita, el vaivén del bambú:
cada beso transformaba hasta hundir las estelas de la luna.
El tiempo no transcurría, se dejaba entreabrir cada noche como
   germen de lo cercano
hasta anular el volumen de otra presencia bajo la fortaleza de los
   párpados.
Cada noche, al cambiar sus espadas de algas,
nombres y formas se sacudían en la penetración
y caían en añicos por el angosto pasillo del olvido.
—Porque no había sido puesto el espejo ni el espejo estaba en los
   pozos falsos,
era posible pensar que hacía sí venía una saeta;
era el eco andrógino, la delectación,
deseos no cumplidos que hablaban como una costumbre de ángeles
o de sombras sin ataduras.

2.

That rapture was the desert's test, the lightning flash that moved
    toward ashy waters
—in the ephemeral garden, roots of thistle, dance of confident leaves,
humid, arboreal roofs warped with the petals that bend in the house
    of wind.
Eros played—in a gesture becoming night's mask,
hell's truant.
Touch was shot through with opulence
and the embrace was the infinite branch, the swaying of bamboo:
each kiss transforming till it sunk in the wake of the moon.
Time wasn't passing, it left itself half-open each night like a germ of
    nearness
to annul the volume of some other presence behind the eyelid's force.
Each night, to transform their algal swords,
names and forms shook with penetration
and fell to pieces in the narrow hallways of forgetting.
—Because the mirror had not been hung nor could it be found in
    false wells,
it was possible to think his arrow was advancing;
it was the androgynous echo, the delectation,
unsatisfied desires which spoke like the voices of angels
or of shadows come undone.

3.

Pero las preguntas conocen sus respuestas—
la que inquietaba, habitaba lo incompleto
y día a día estaba en las imágenes vacías
hasta que la llama alumbró la identidad,
ahora tránsito hacia la huida.

Entonces, lo que la luz descubrió, no fue el rostro
—estaba en la muerte y era parte de las vestiduras,
de los pasos que, intranquilos y leves, acosaron aun desde los muros.
El sueño vino aquí a deshacerse, rompió sus lazos, abrió los pliegues.

Lo que la luz fue a descubrir no era el reconocimiento
sino el propio rasguño, la fosa donde las palabras habitan
—ningún rumor como esa escarcha, su halo en la posesión.
Cuando Eros-espectro ahuyenta las manchas moradas,
no ve la trampa —soy lo mismo, sin vehemencia,
mas no era antes de este lugar y este deseo.

Lo que la luz fue a descubrir estaba en el tiempo,
bosque de brumas.
Memoria de hilos dorados, sutiles como nubes, firmes como rocas:
otro es lo necesario —con sed se demora.
Nada vendrá a este hueco, las agujas clavan el vacío,
el alma opaca habla o se diluye
—la semejanza, Psique, en las borrascas.
Ojos para ver el fin del puente de Narciso.

3.

But the questions contain their answers—
unsettled, she dwelled in the unfinished
each day in the empty images
until the flame illuminated identity,
now a path to escape.

So that what the light discovered was not the face
—it was death's and of death's clothing,
of the steps which, anxious and light, hound with their echoes.
The dream came here to unmake itself, broke its bonds, opened the
    folds.

What light went in search of wasn't memory
but its own sketch, the pit where words live
—silent like the frost, possession as its halo.
When ghost-Eros banishes the purple stains,
he doesn't see the trap—I'm the same, without vehemence,
but not before this place and this desire.

What light went in search of was in time,
forest of haze.
Memory of golden threads, thin like clouds, hard like rocks:
necessity is other—with thirst it delays.
Nothing will fill this space, needles thread the void,
the opaque soul speaks or dissolves
—the likeness, Psyche, in the squalls.
Eyes with which to see the end of Narcissus's bridge.

Alegoría de la mañana

1.

Un rayo de luz, Thomas Carew,
que aún no comience. Ningún rumor,
el silencio de ausentes detalles,
un aire desgranado.

No hay todavía tiempo —el sueño suspende al cuerpo en sus lazos
y él se hunde en el resto de la noche.

El beso áspero e indiferente
vendrá con su látigo en el galope de la locura
tan imaginaria como la razón que dice regir,
mientras ella, la anunciadora de la fuerza,
aparece bajo pliegues que crujen suavemente.

Cautela en la hora del pájaro.
Entra también el ángel llevando su cuchillo
y corta en el cuerpo sin sangre
—transforma al doble en el doble de sí.
Un rayo de luz, Thomas Carew.

Allegory of the Morning

1.

Un rayo de luz, Thomas Carew,
which still has not begun. No murmur,
the silence of absent details,
a threshed air.

There is not yet time—the dream suspends the body in its nets
and it sinks into the remainder of the night.

The rough and indifferent kiss
will come with its whip in the gallop of madness
as imaginary as the reason that claims to rule,
while madness, the mouthpiece of force,
appears beneath gently intersecting folds.

Caution in the hour of the bird.
The angel too enters carrying its knife
and cuts into the bloodless body
—transforming the double into a double of itself.
Un rayo de luz, Thomas Carew.

2.

¿Y ese resplandor no está también en la ruina
y la ruina de la memoria atravesada por infinitos deseos de olvido y
su negación
—hundir la mirada y alimentar otros sentidos en el espejismo del
miedo?

Atrás, el viajero bordea las orillas de una tierra cercana vista en otro
tiempo
—tanto hecho en la sombra y urdido en la sombra donde prueba la
exaltación y la duda.
La servidumbre de la mente es una ley amarga.
El cuerpo es un Leteo ávido de tacto.

2.

And isn't that brightness also in the ruins
and aren't the ruins of memory crisscrossed by infinite desires of
    oblivion and its negation
—to collapse the gaze and nourish other senses in fear's mirage?

Behind, the traveler skirts the shore of a neighboring land seen in
    another time
—so formed in shadow and warped in shadow where it tests
    exaltation and doubt.
The mind's bondage is a bitter law.
The body a Lethe eager for touch.

3.

Suena la hora de la adormidera.
¿Vendrá sobre esta única mañana que, como un alba menor,
asesta dardos de neblina?

Y suena las seis.
Es la hora de la adormidera,
meciéndome —lo fecundo es sereno, está oculto,
la tierra húmeda, silenciosa.

3.

The poppy's hour sounds.
Will it come on this unique morning that, like a minor dawn,
delivers darts of fog?

Six chimes.
It's the poppy's hour,
I'm swaying—the fecund is serene, it's hidden,
the humid, silent earth.

Casa como reino

Oyendo a mis hijos hablar y balbucear

Ella pronuncia sílabas, vocales, sin imitación,
cede a su propio fluido el placer de sonidos crecientes,
gritos, aullidos, que la acercan al sueño animal.
Persistencia, pienso, niña exploradora en la canción o el lamento.

Él construye hondos fosos o torres en el atrio de un bosque
labrado cuidadosamente: tono, justeza, afecto.
Descalzo en el profundo canal, alimentándose en las redecillas
encantadas a la hora en que los labios vienen
de un país amoroso.

Ella en el fluido de la palabra, él en el acecho de la palabra,
mientras arrojo mi indagación:
¿viniste, árbol que puedes hablarles, a mirar cómo se atan
lentamente al límite, como si el gozo debiera ser
arrancado a la corrección?
¿y viniste tú, sonido, a darles tu decir diurno, vestido de duende
de voces?

House as Kingdom

Hearing my children talk and babble

She pronounces syllables, vowels, without imitation,
ceding to its own movement the pleasure of growing sound,
   little shouts, howls, which draw her into the animal dream.
Persistence, I think, daughter explorer in the song or the lament.

He builds deep pits or towers in the atrium of a forest
   carefully wrought: tone, justness, feeling.
Barefoot in the deep canal, feeding in the enchanted reticula the
   hour lips arrive from an amorous country.

She in the current of the word, he in the ambush of the word,
while I discard my inquiry.
Did you come, tree of speech, to see how they bind themselves
   slowly to the limits, as if pleasure should be
   wrestled from correctness?
And did you come, sound, to give them your daily speech, dressed in
   the charm of voices?

Cuando escucho...

Cuando escucho que se parten las ramas,
cuando los arrullo en ese espacio sin género ni nombre,
cuando oprimo mi carne contra las suyas,
   sin compartir, sin penetrar

cuando me oyen, cuando los oigo
despojados, leves,
luz nocturna, luz solar,
aureola —el cielo invisible desde la ventana,
estribillos sin equilibrio,
hierba, olor, río

cuando me levanto, cuando como,
cuando, sumergida en el unicornio, mascullo mi envejecimiento
   o transito sombras de cabellos, de árboles, de huesos,
cuando los despierto, cuando duermo,
los gestos son usuales, los cuerpos se asemejan,
   o se mezclan en ese rincón vacío, hasta reconocer
     mi mirada

y en el filo del día, ato la repetición, ato las voces
—ninguno de nosotros ve la necesidad transparente,
esa lengua sin comienzo ni final,
para sobros de intrusos

When I hear...

When I hear the branches breaking,
when I coo to them in that space without name or gender,
when I press my flesh against theirs
   without sharing, without penetrating

when they hear me, when I hear them
stripped, slight,
light of the moon, light of the sun,
halo—the sky invisible from the window,
chorus without balance,
grass, smell, river

when I get up, when I eat,
when, immersed as the unicorn, I grumble my aging
   or travel the shadows of horses, trees, bones,
when I wake them, when I sleep,
the gestures are common, the bodies mirrored,
   or they intermix in that empty corner, until recognizing
     my gaze

and on the edge of day, I gather repetition, I gather the voices
—none of us see the transparent need,
that endless language,
for a gulp of invasion

Leer...

Leer se pierde en la transformación de la letra.
Lo que está (se deshace como polvo de nieve)
deifican algunos, la mano con confianza
de amigos distantes —es una certeza.
Otros absorben el relato de ropajes reales
—la veracidad como privilegio para pedir lo imposible:
un hombre y su tiempo mutuamente emparentados.

Y esa naturaleza ahora extraña
como una casa encantada,
está envuelta en cristales.

Para mí, los semblantes poseídos duran infinitas estaciones.
No me cansan los sueños que olvido en el musgo.
La belleza insiste en un principio diáfano,
cautiva en silenciosos ecos, tonos
—puedo transportarme hasta los miembros locuaces
    de la observación
y atravesar esa puerta de abstinencia:
la que hace la perspectiva de la letra, su exclusión de la muerte.

Reading...

Reading you lose yourself in the transformation of the text.
What's there (it dissolves like a dusting of snow)
glorifies some, their hands confident as those
of distant friends—it's a certainty.
Others absorb the story of royal robes
—truth as a privilege to request the impossible:
a man and his time linked reciprocally.

And that now strange nature
like an enchanted house
is wrapped in crystals.

For me, the faces I ponder last for infinite seasons.
The dreams I forget in the moss don't exhaust me.
Beauty insists on a diaphanous beginning,
captive in silent echoes, tones
—I can carry myself to the loquacious aspects
          of observation
and pass through that door of abstinence:
the one that shapes the letter's perspective, its negation of death.

Ritos cotidianos...

Ritos cotidianos, sobre una manta adversa, sin mancha ni alas.

Se esparcen los objetos, van como piedras vivientes,
oscuro el salón, el pozo lleno.

No había hastío —iba más allá
como un luto hecho para los relámpagos diurnos:
casa, mano, helecho.
¿Quién al fin del día?
Reglas como brazaletes,
agujas azules en la puerta.

Voy a buscar mi nombre, ahora oculto entre la fuente y el arco
—pero el arco de yeso es un pórtico para islas, saltos con andamios.

Guardiana de día; por las noches, sombra:
es mi deseo la peregrinación del árbol.
En su corteza mi historia se cubre de moho, de estiércol
—lo que fui no me obedece.

Quotidian rites...

Quotidian rites, above an unfavorable blanket, with neither stains
    nor wings.

The objects disperse, they move like living stones,
the room dark, the full well.

There was no boredom—it went beyond
like a lament for daytime lightning:
house, hand, fern.
Who at the day's end?
Rules like bracelets,
blue needles in the door.

I go in search of my name, now hidden between the fountain and
    the arc
—but the arc of bone is a portico for islands, scaffolded waterfalls.

Guardian of the day, shadow of the night:
my desire is the tree's pilgrimage.
In its bark my story covers itself with moss, with dung
—what I was does not obey me.

Sobre la quietud

Línea en suspenso, áurea de bruma,
espesor, oculta diafanidad, intensidad.
Pero, ¿de qué instancia es la fuerza? ¿de qué medida?
Reminiscencia de los telones de hule de la infancia:
por fin sin miedo, sin espera.

No a la pasión (tan sólo como beso soñado).
Ausentar el cuerpo, suspenderlo —el goce del no-sentir:
he ahí la luminosidad del lenguaje que no puede pensarse.
Herida de las palabras, carbón, agujero—
las metáforas que machacan o tajean el hilillo de las voces
—cadenas.
La metáfora que reincide como maldición.

Y ahora el lenguaje como trama de muerte y de posibles,
su inasibilidad, la caducidad de lo dicho,
lo inhallable de lo escrito:
boca y voz no pueden encontrarse.

Above the calm

Line suspended, goldenness of fog,
thickness, hidden transparency, intensity.
But, what request issues its strength? Of what size?
Reminiscence of the rubber cloths of infancy:
finally without fear, without hope.

No to passion (as lonesome as the kiss of dreams).
To absent the body, suspend it—the pleasure of not feeling:
I have here the luminosity of language unable to reflect on itself.
Wound of words, carbon, holes—
the metaphors that crush or cut the little thread of voices
    —chains.
The metaphor that relapses like a curse.

And now language like the plot of death and possibilities,
its ungraspability, the expiration of the spoken,
the undiscoverable of what's written:
mouth and voice cannot find each other.

Fudekara

Fudekara

Día 1

En un rincón me senté a la luz de la lámpara. Ya era tarde y todos habían comenzado a trabajar.

Estaba el papel, estaba la tinta. Escaso silencio —pensé, mientras oía el murmullo.

Sensei me dio unas notas, y empecé a leer.

Day 1

In a corner I sat in the light of the lamp. Already it was late and the others had begun to work.

There was paper, there was ink. Scarce silence—I thought, though I could hear the rustling.

Sensei gave me some notes, and I began to read.

Día 2

Los signos multiplican los instantes. El signo y la repetición forman una corriente de confianza, de liberación. En esa corriente debo aprender a ahogar la ansiedad. Imagino un nuevo lugar en la mente que nace de este punto material, duro, pétreo. Es un punto inorgánico e indefinido, como lo que inicia la posibilidad. El comienzo de la posibilidad no es aún el comienzo.

Esta noche, el ojo reemplazará al oído. El ojo reemplazará a la respiración.

Day 2

The signs multiply the moments. The sign and its repetition form a current of trust, of liberation. In that current I should learn to drown my anxiety. I imagine a new space in the mind, born from this material point, tough and rocky. It's an inorganic, undefined point, like the beginning of a possibility. The beginning of possibility is not even the beginning.

Tonight, sound will be replaced by the eye. Breath will be replaced by the eye.

Día 3

El viaje de regreso ya tiene su mapa. Supervivencia en aguas de azúcar, ritmo de algas.

La tierra en la hondonada quebrándose —conocía por la cabeza, y en la mente, insectos revoloteaban y recorrían la ciudad de tu mapa.

Labraba en la montaña materia de mar.

Un nuevo trópico dividiría los días —pensé. Los días al azar comenzaban otra vez, como cardúmenes de arcilla, en la costa.

Conocía por la cabeza, y deambulaba por la ciudad de tu mapa.

Day 3

The return trip has a map already. Surviving in sugar waters, in rhythms of algae.

The earth in the hollow is breaking—I knew through my skull, and in my mind, insects were swarming, traversing the city of your map.

I carved into the mountain of ocean things.

I thought: A new tropic would divide the days. The days had begun again randomly, like shoals of clay, on the coast.

I knew through my skull, and I was wandering the city of your map.

Día 4

No es el trazo mi obsesión, sino esto actuado que se inicia a la madrugada, como un insomnio puesto en la luz de imágenes de ayer, de otra tarde.

Me impongo un exilio en redes de polvo, me ahogo (pero ocultándome en la indiferencia).

En realidad, multiplico mi cuerpo, multiplico mi mente, y donde tenía brazo y mano, y donde había sed, abandono la idea de persona.

Day 4

My obsession isn't the stroke, but the stroke enacted, which begins with the dawn, with an insomnia set in the light of yesterday's images, of a different afternoon.

I exile myself in webs of dust, I drown myself (but hide in the indifference).

No: I multiply my body, I multiply my mind, and where there was arm and hand, and where there was thirst, I abandon the idea of person.

Diá 5

En silencio, dibujo fragmentos de signos, trazos, como ejercicios.

Al repetir, empecé a olvidar mi mano. Pero aún el camino será exterior por mucho tiempo.

La curva refugia maneras de envolver el blanco.

Day 5

In silence, I sketch fragments of signs, strokes, like exercises.

Through repetition, I began to forget my hand. But even the path will be foreign before long.

The curve shelters ways of shrouding the white.

Día 6

Inestable la conducta; acaso como escudo mi pincel se suelta en respuestas a la luna.

Persigo una habitación imposible, conceder lo dicho a otro oído, a otra ley.

Day 6

Behavior unsteady; perhaps as a defense, my brush loosens itself in answers to the moon.

I chase an impossible room, to concede the spoken to another ear, another rule.

Día 7

Ejercitación sobre el trazo aunque los signos son desconocidos.

Alguien apoya la mano en el tintero y la tinta crece.

Mi párpado se he negado. El párpado se cierra y utiliza la fuerza de ese hilo que sabe que está, que ya lo ha atado.

La sombra del atardecer sobre el río es leve, algo terrosa, de un gris cambiante y espeso. El río se dibuja también leve, sin orígenes.

Alguien apoya la mano en el tintero y gira la barra en círculos, en curvas lentas.

Corté entonces mi mente, la atravesé con una línea de vidrio.

Liberaba la explicación al sentimiento de lo impropio, al mundo tácito.

Sabía que había entrado en el tiempo —y el tiempo se abriría en sendas, y en cada senda sería otra.

Day 7

Practicing the stroke though the signs are unknown.

Someone rests the hand on the inkwell and the ink rises.

My eyelid has refused. The eyelid closes, using the force of the knowing thread which has already stitched it shut.

The shadow of dusk over the river is slight, something muddy, of a thick and shifting gray. The river too draws itself lightly, without origins.

Someone rests the hand on the inkwell and spins the bar in circles, slow curves.

Then I cut my mind, I pierced it with a line of glass.

I was liberating reason to the feeling of the improper, to the unspoken world.

I knew that I had entered time—and that time would fork into paths, and on each path I would be another.

Día 8

Noche de tormenta. La tormenta no está en el cielo o en el aire, sino que viaja en raíces, de soplo en soplo en lo animado, y va dibujando puertas.

Es el hechizo de esta hora tambaleante bajo la corriente de una sangre simbólica.

Debo inventar otra mano. Como en un baile, hacer movimientos de coreografía sabidos, ponerse en el puente que va del saber a la acción.

Ausente estaba en el ascenso —mi oído se dejaba encantar.

Nunca me soltaré de estas amarras.

La boca se sella en el agua, inesperado grito se acalla en los pedazos de las palabras. Nada se mueve, sin embargo.

La tormenta desgaja el anochecer de septiembre, lo convierte en instantes de ansiedad, de espera, de huellas vacías —que ya superias cómo la curva desemboca en el silencio, cómo el negro acuoso hace ramas de sauce y el negro intenso se agrieta en rocas y nubes.

Hacia el oeste, los árboles metállicos quedaron quietos —iban por pasadizos rozando el aire. Bajo la piel entró la luz lunar. Entró y fue el principio —no quiere que recuerde y resguarda en la oscuridad esta tela insípida y dolorosa.

Day 8

Night of storms. Not in the sky or the air, but a storm that travels in roots, from breath to breath in the living, painting doors.

It's the spell of this unsteady hour beneath the flow of a symbolic blood.

I should invent another hand. As in a dance, to make the known movements of choreography, to place yourself on the bridge between thought and action.

Absent it was in the ascent—my hearing allowed its enchantment.

Never will I free myself from these moorings.

The mouth seals itself in water, the unwanted shout silenced in fragments of words. And yet nothing moves.

The storm splits dusk from September, converting it into moments of anxiety, of delay, of empty traces—that you knew already how the curve flows into silence, how the watery blackness makes willow branches and the powerful blackness cracks in rocks and clouds.

Towards the west, metallic trees stayed motionless—they were moving through alleys, brushing the air. Beneath the skin, the lunar light entered. It entered and was the beginning—not wanting to remember and shielding in the blackness this insipid and painful cloth.

Día 9

Con los manos extendidas, la ciudad absoluta deja una estela en el ojo. La ciudad se troquela y cada parte entra en el pasado. Ahora lo elude la desolación, el inesperado demonio que apresó, como un caballo que embistiera el cielo. Y en la puna del pincel, la atmósfera se resiste.

Sensei sonríe —defensa contra la vida del rey, y en su vientre el tatuaje del perro.

Inesperadamente dramática sonríe y empuja la conversación al deshielo.

No habrá ceremonia.

De diversos y lejanos lugares son la cenizas que traías en la cajita y que dejaste que se expandieran, que fueran otro dibujo tallado en la segunda puerta.

Repito y repite ideograma o rasgo.

No habrá ceremonia.

La caja está en mis manos y su piedra es el entonces para nosotros, este jueves, este jueves tejido en los árboles.

¿Por qué escribir las confesiones?

¿Por qué confesar lo escrito?

Day 9

With hands outstretched, the absolute city leaves a wake in the eye. The city divides itself into coins and each part enters the past. Now desolation, the capture of that unexpected demon, eludes it, as a horse would charge the sky. And on the tip of the brush, the atmosphere resists.

Sensei smiles—a defense against the king's life, and on her belly the tattoo of the dog.

Unexpectedly and dramatically she smiles and pushes the conversation to a thaw.

There will be no ceremony.

From diverse and distant places are the ashes that you brought in the little box and that you left to spread, which were another picture carved into the second door.

I repeat and she repeats ideogram or stroke.

There will be no ceremony.

The box is in my hands and its rock is the then for us, this Thursday, this Thursday woven in the trees.

Why write confessions?

Why confess the written?

Día 10

Al escribir, observo. Después, voy hacia tierras marcadas con signos invisibles. Cierro los ojos y entro en la gruta. Me esperás para darme el mapa. Sabía que tu mapa era el deseado.

Cierro los ojos, porque el tiempo se ha dividido en tantos hilos...

Como un nuevo cielo, el aire envuelve la gruta.

Tu mapa crece y me muestra el árbol y su sombra. El árbol también crece y estás en sus hojas, que como brazos, me sostienen.

Palmo a palmo recorro la tierra leída.

Day 10

While writing, I observe. After, I travel through lands marked with invisible signs. I close my eyes and enter into the cave. You're waiting for me, to give me the map. I knew it was your map that I came for.

I close my eyes, because time has divided itself into so many threads...

Like a new sky, the air envelopes the cave.

Your map is growing, it shows me a tree and its shadow. The tree too is growing and you're in its leaves which, like arms, support me.

Bit by bit I travel the well-read lands.

Día 11

Monotonía. Del pedazo, buscar otro pedazo. De él, otro. Al ir dividiendo el espacio y el tiempo, el ojo se va alejando, hasta que el blanco ocupa la mano.

Delante del papel, el torso inclinado, el brazo alargado. Pero mi mente se ata demasiado a la madera.

El río, línea mansa, crea un horizonte móvil.

Day 11

Monotony. From one piece, to search for another piece. From him, another. To progress, dividing space and time, the eye distancing itself until blankness occupies the hand.

In front of the paper, the body inclined, the arm extended. But my mind is too tied to the wood.

The river, steady line, creates a moving horizon.

Día 12

De la dirección de la fuerza puede inferirse una virtud. Resistir, en otra dirección, permite descubrir la imitación, la parodia. Pero ahora no puede más que permanecer en el centro, considerar la nebulosa del hábito.

No sé agazaparme como animal, o como flor, gradualmente cerrar hojas orgánicas.

Las palabras apoyadas en la garganta, áridas, perdidas, se adelgazan. La mirada esquiva se apresura a no modelar el aire y se evapora.

Escribo cada trazo sin guía. Escribo morosamente.

Day 12

From the direction of the force you can deduce a virtue. To resist, in the other direction, allows you to discover imitation, parody. But for now you can only remain in the center, considering the nebula of habit.

I don't know how to crouch like an animal, or like a flower, to gradually close my organic leaves.

The words resting in the throat—arid, lost—are thinning. The distant glance evaporates, rushing so as not to mold the air.

I write each stroke without a guide. I write slowly, like a debtor.

Día 13

La fuerza del trazo no debo detenerse. La fuerza recorre el brazo y allí se absorbe. Sin apoyar el brazo —la mano en el aire, y la fuerza como aliento de éter sólido. Que allí se forme una sombra rígida, madera sin paisaje —aunque el paisaje es lo buscado en la oscuridad de la sala.

En un vaso de agua se esconderá esta estación tan larga, o se doblará con el viento sobre el río.

Esperaré el corazón animal.

Esperaré el comienzo del día, y aun sin voz, hablaré para vos.

Day 13

The force of the stroke should not be stopped. The force runs through the arm and is absorbed there. Without supporting the arm—the hand in the air, and the force like a breath of solid ether. That there it forms a rigid shadow, wood without landscape—though it's the landscape that's sought in the darkness of the room.

In a glass of water this long season will hide itself, or it will bend with the wind above the river.

I will wait for the animal heart.

I will wait for dawn, and even without voice, I will speak for you.

Día 14

Fantasmas cambian la mano. Tu voz es emocional, desmedida. El relato razona en la memoria. No desmiente la sed, lo fugaz, la bravura del mar, el perfil de los árboles, la sombra de la roca.

Fantasmas cambian los ojos. Amenazan ceñir otro cuerpo a la cabeza.

Tu voz ha creado hilos que crecen en las pupilas.

Escribo. Escribo signos. Escribo muerta. Escribo otra. Escribo para no hablar, para no mirar.

Day 14

Spirits change the hand. Your voice is emotional, excessive. The story reasons in memory. It doesn't deny the thirst, what's fleeting, the ferocity of the sea, the profile of the trees, the shadow of the rock.

Spirits change the eyes. They threaten to bind another body to the skull.

Your voice has formed threads that grow in the pupils.

I write. I write signs. I write death. I write another. I write so I don't have to speak, so I don't have to watch.

Este texto fue escrito durante el transcurso de las clases de caligrafía de ideogramas chinos, a cargo de la profesora Alicia N. Li, que tuvieron lugar en la Sección de Estudios Interdisciplinarios de Asia y África de la Universidad de Buenos Aires, durante los meses de septiembre y octubre de 1993.

La escritura del idioma japonés utiliza ideogramas chinos (*kanji*), combinándolos con caracteres hiragana y katakana.

El término fudekara (fudékará) es una libre asociación que realicé relacionando los términos en japonés *fude* y *kara*, "pincel" y "desde," respectivamente—, con el orden sintáctico habitual en esa lengua.

—L.P.

This text was written during a Chinese ideograph calligraphy class led by Professor Alicia N. Li, which was held in the Department of Interdisciplinary Asian and African Studies at the University of Buenos Aires, during the months of September and October, 1993.

Japanese language script uses Chinese ideographs (*kanji*), combining them with *hiragana* and *katakana* characters.

The term *fudekara* (fudékará) is a neologism created by connecting the Japanese terms *fude* and *kara*, "brush" and "from," respectively—in the syntactical order typical of the language.

—L.P.

Acknowledgments

The sections "La estación sombría," "Más allá de la estación sombría," "Sólo el ojo ve el azul," "El conocimiento siembra el cuerpo," "Diario," and "Otras poemas" were first published as *Teoría de la voz y el sueño* (Buenos Aires: tsé-tsé, 2001). "Fudekara" was first published as *Fudekara* (Buenos Aires: tsé-tsé, 2008).

"Diario/Diary" was published as a bilingual chapbook by Ugly Duckling Presse in 2018. Gracious thanks to the UDP editorial team, especially Katherine Bogden, Silvina López Medin, and Rebekah Smith, whose assistance with the manuscript was invaluable, and whose early guidance helped me to become a more thoughtful and observant translator. "Fudekara" was published as a bilingual chapbook by Cardboard House Press in 2022. Thank you to the editors—Giancarlo Huapaya and Charlotte Whittle—for helping to steward this project into the world. Thank you as well to Joyelle McSweeney, Valerie Mejer Caso, Cecilia Vicuña, and Lila Zemborain for their words of support for these early volumes, and to Maxime Berclaz, Tobias Carroll, Paul Cunningham, and Roz Naimi for their thoughtful and generous reviews.

Earlier versions of individual poems have appeared in *Asymptote*, *Denver Quarterly*, *Guernica*, *Gulf Coast*, *New England Review*, and *Poetry*. Thank you to the editors who believed in these pieces. A special thank you is owed to the editorial team at *New England Review* and David Francis in particular, for offering me the opportunity to reflect on my practice as a translator. This is a stronger book because of our conversation.

Theory of the Voice and Dream began almost a decade ago as the inkling of an idea, and has been stewarded along by numerous friends, colleagues, and mentors who deserve mention: the late Kent Johnson, who offered invaluable guidance and support when I was an aimless poet and nascent translator; Reynaldo Jiménez, whose generosity and friendship in Buenos Aires made me feel at home; Juan Pablo Ferrer and Rodrigo Mirto, for providing a home base in La Plata at Residencia Corazón; Emily Wilson, a passionate advocate for translation and a model of creative scholarship whose support and enthusiasm for this project helped keep it within my sightline when other responsibilities threatened to crowd it out; my colleagues in Comparative Literature at Penn, especially India Halstead and Zain Mian, who in conversation and critique helped deepen my engagement with the work;

Alexis Almeida and Jake Syersak for various forms of encouragement and support over the years, as well as (unbeknownst to me) editing the finished manuscript. At some point in the last decade, I acquired the irritating habit of firing off a draft of whatever I'm working on to friends as soon as I am even mildly proud of it; thank you to Marty Cain and Evan Gray, the primary recipients of these messages, without whose friendship I would not be a writer of any kind today. Thank you to Matvei Yankelevich and World Poetry Books for giving this project a home.

    A special thank you to my wife, Maegan, whose contributions to this project—to my life—are beyond number. I completed a first draft of this book the month before we learned that our son, Parker, would be joining our family, and finished the final edits just before his second birthday—thanks, bub.

    Finally, it goes without saying that this book would not exist if Liliana Ponce did not exist, not only as the author of these pieces but as a model for what it means to live the poet's life. Gracias por todo—abrazo enorme.

Liliana Ponce (b. 1950) is a poet and scholar of Japanese literature and writing. She has published five full-length books of poetry in Argentina. A selected volume of her poems was published in Colombia in 2019. She is also a translator of Japanese poetry and drama, and served as editor for an anthology of Japanese Noh plays. Her poems, essays, and translations have appeared in literary journals and anthologies both in Argentina and internationally, including in the pages of the seminal hemispheric magazine *Mandorla: Nueva escritura de las Américas/New Writing from the Americas*. She lives in Buenos Aires.

Michael Martin Shea is a poet, translator, editor, and literary critic. His translation of Liliana Ponce's *Diary* was published as a bilingual chapbook by Ugly Duckling Presse; a second chapbook, *Fudekara*, was published by Cardboard House Press. Shea is also the author of five chapbooks of poetry and hybrid writing. His poems and translations have appeared in *Chicago Review*, *Conjunctions*, *Denver Quarterly*, *Fence*, *Guernica*, *jubilat*, *New England Review*, *Poetry*, and elsewhere. A former Fulbright Fellow to Argentina, he is currently an assistant professor of English at the University of Louisiana at Lafayette.

This book was typeset in Alegreya and Alegreya Sans, twenty-first-century typefaces inspired by humanist and calligraphic design traditions. Both were designed by Juan Pablo del Peral for Huerta Tipográfica, Buenos Aires. The cover, designed by Andrew Bourne, is adapted from the artwork of Argentine painter Gabriela Giusti. Typesetting by Don't Look Now. Printed and bound in Lithuania by BALTO Print. Manufactured by Arctic Paper in Sweden, the paper in this book meets EU Ecolabel, Forest Stewardship Council, and Cradle to Cradle certification standards.

 WORLD POETRY

Marie-Noëlle Agniau
The Escapades
tr. Jesse Hover Amar

Nadia Anjuman
Smoke Drifts: Selected Poems
tr. Diana Arterian & Marina Omar

Jean-Paul Auxeméry
Selected Poems
tr. Nathaniel Tarn

Boethius
The Poems from On the Consolation of Philosophy
tr. Peter Glassgold

Maria Borio
Transparencies
tr. Danielle Pieratti

Astrid Cabral
Spotlight on the Word
tr. Alexis Levitin

Jeannette L. Clariond
Goddesses of Water
tr. Samantha Schnee

Jacques Darras
John Scotus Eriugena at Laon
tr. Richard Sieburth

Mario dell'Arco
Day Lasts Forever: Selected Poems
tr. Marc Alan Di Martino

Marie de Quatrebarbes
The Vitals
tr. Aiden Farrell

Olivia Elias
Chaos, Crossing
tr. Kareem James Abu-Zeid

Gastón Fernández
Apparent Breviary
tr. KM Cascia

Jerzy Ficowski
Everything I Don't Know
tr. Jennifer Grotz & Piotr Sommer
PEN AWARD FOR POETRY IN TRANSLATION

Antonio Gamoneda
Book of the Cold
tr. Katherine M. Hedeen & Víctor Rodríguez Núñez

Mireille Gansel
Soul House
tr. Joan Seliger Sidney

Óscar García Sierra
Houston, I'm the problem
tr. Carmen Yus Quintero

Phoebe Giannisi
Homerica
tr. Brian Sneeden

Zuzanna Ginczanka
On Centaurs & Other Poems
tr. Alex Braslavsky

Julien Gracq
Abounding Freedom
tr. Alice Yang

Leeladhar Jagoori
What of the Earth Was Saved
tr. Matt Reeck

*Nakedness Is My End:
Poems from the Greek Anthology*
tr. Edmund Keeley

Birhan Keskin
Earthly Conditions: Selected Poems
tr. Öykü Tekten

Jazra Khaleed
The Light That Burns Us
ed. Karen Van Dyck

Judith Kiros
O
tr. Kira Josefsson

Dimitra Kotoula
The Slow Horizon That Breathes
tr. Maria Nazos

Maria Laina
Hers
tr. Karen Van Dyck

Maria Laina
Rose Fear
tr. Sarah McCann

Perrin Langda
A Few Microseconds on Earth
tr. Pauline Levy Valensi

Anna Malihon
Girl with a Bullet
tr. Olena Jennings

Afrizal Malna
Document Shredding Museum
tr. Daniel Owen

Joyce Mansour
In the Glittering Maw: Selected Poems
tr. C. Francis Fisher

Manuel Maples Arce
Stridentist Poems
tr. KM Cascia

Ennio Moltedo
Night
tr. Marguerite Feitlowitz

Meret Oppenheim
The Loveliest Vowel Empties: Collected Poems
tr. Kathleen Heil

Giovanni Pascoli
Last Dream
tr. Geoffrey Brock
RAIZISS/DE PALCHI TRANSLATION AWARD

Gabriel Pomerand
Saint Ghetto of the Loans
tr. Michael Kasper &
Bhamati Viswanathan

Liliana Ponce
Theory of the Voice and Dream
tr. Michael Martin Shea

Rainer Maria Rilke
Where the Paths Do Not Go
tr. Burton Pike

Amelia Rosselli
Document
tr. Roberta Antognini & Deborah Woodard

Elisabeth Rynell
Night Talks
tr. Rika Lesser

Waly Salomão
Border Fare
tr. Maryam Monalisa Gharavi

George Sarantaris
Abyss and Song: Selected Poems
tr. Pria Louka

George Seferis
Book of Exercises II
tr. Jennifer R. Kellogg

Seo Jung Hak
The Cheapest France in Town
tr. Megan Sungyoon

Ahmad Shamlou
Elegies of the Earth: Selected Poems
tr. Niloufar Talebi

Ardengo Soffici
Simultaneities & Lyric Chemisms
tr. Olivia E. Sears

Liesl Ujvary
Good & Safe
tr. Ann Cotten & Anna-Isabella Dinwoodie

Paul Verlaine
Before Wisdom: The Early Poems
tr. Keith Waldrop & K.A. Hays

Witold Wirpsza
Apotheosis of Music
tr. Frank L. Vigoda

Uljana Wolf
kochanie, today i bought bread
tr. Greg Nissan

Ye Lijun
My Mountain Country
tr. Fiona Sze-Lorrain

Verónica Zondek
Cold Fire
tr. Katherine Silver